GREAT
CHRISTMAS MOVIES

GREAT CHRISTMAS MOVIES

Holiday Favorites
Behind-the-Scenes
Fun & Trivia

by Elizabeth Haynie

Anton Publications
Downers Grove, Illinois

Published by Anton Publications
PO Box 606, Downers Grove, IL 60516 USA

Printed in the United States of America

ISBN 0-9637195-4-8

TABLE OF CONTENTS

INTRODUCTION

It's hard to imagine there was a time when people celebrated Christmas without a tree, but before Great Britain's Queen Victoria popularized this German tradition, no one outside Germany decorated a tree. And it's just as hard to believe there was a time when the Christmas season wasn't marked by watching favorite holiday movies on television. Hollywood, of course, had been putting Christmas scenes in movies since the early days of movies. Versions of the life of Christ had been made even in the days of silent pictures, and Dickens' *Christmas Carol* attracted filmmakers in the early days of talkies.

But Christmas movies as we know them--the kind that are telecast each year between Thanksgiving and Christmas and that began showing up on videocassette and DVD in the early days of each medium--really began in 1942 with *Holiday Inn*. Not only did this film introduce the great Christmas song "White Christmas," it practically served as a template for every Christmas film that followed.

Holiday Inn featured the now-familiar snow-covered scenery, the picturesque towns and cities of an idealized America, the emphasis on holiday feasting and finery, and the testing of the leading man's character. By the end of almost every Christmas movie, the leading man rediscovers the importance of friends and family and gains a new joy in living.

Of course, the classic Christmas movies rarely make any direct reference to Christmas as an important Christian holiday, but the spirit is there. The timeless qualities of unselfishness, kindness, and humility are invariably contrasted with the shallowness of more worldly goals, with the former emerging as the clear winners. Moviegoers are meant to feel uplifted and optimistic at the end of a Christmas movie. Holiday movies that attempt to reach that goal but fail never make the status of a classic.

This book is filled with those that *have* become classics. Yes, it's true that the older films are warmer and more sincere. As much as we may love *A Christmas Story* or laugh at *National Lampoon's Christmas Vacation*, the slightly cynical tone of each of these films leaves the viewer in no doubt that they weren't made during the Golden Years of Hollywood. But even these films capture the spirit of the Christmas season in making us take a look at ourselves and our own holiday obsessions and making us laugh in the process.

Of course, any selection of the "best" is bound to be controversial but most true film buffs love a good argument, anyway. For me, the films in this book make the grade because there are memorable scenes, true-to-life characters, lines of dialogue I find myself repeating again and again--and because they create that tingling feeling of anticipation that Christmas day is drawing nearer. Each one may not be a masterpiece, but I hope you'll agree that each of them contains the essence of what makes Christmas movies great.

IT'S A WONDERFUL LIFE

VITAL STATISTICS
Year Released: 1946
Studio: Liberty/RKO

Director: Frank Capra
Writers: Frank Capra, Frances Goodrich, and Albert Hackett
Cast: James Stewart, Donna Reed, Lionel Barrymore, Thomas
      Mitchell, Beulah Bondi, Ward Bond, and Gloria Grahame

Academy Award Nominations: 5
Academy Awards Won: 0

Claim to Fame: It wasn't a huge hit when it was first released, but it wasn't ignored, either (witness the five Academy Award nominations). Nevertheless, in the three decades after it was made, it faded. Then, in 1973, the copyright expired on this all-but-forgotten film due to a clerical error. That error ensured the film's survival. Suddenly, every television station in America included it in their holiday line-up--after all, it was free. That's when it deservedly--and belatedly--became everybody's favorite holiday movie. Since that time, it has regularly made the lists of "best films ever." Director Frank Capra always knew it was great, though; he always mentioned *It's a Wonderful Life* as his own favorite among his many films.

THE STORY

George Bailey (Jimmy Stewart) is a small-town boy who dreams of being a world traveler and architect. But time after time, his efforts to leave Bedford Falls are thwarted by his own good heart. He runs the family business, but in spite of a happy family life with his wife (Donna Reed), he grows increasingly frustrated. His firm has lost $8,000 and George faces jail. He complains that everybody in his life would be better off if he had never been born. Lucky for George, an angel (Henry Travers) has been sent to show him how wrong he is. The angel shows George how profoundly he has affected people--in fact, he has single-handedly kept the town from being a monument to evil banker Henry Potter (Lionel Barrymore). Realizing that "no man is a failure who has friends," George returns home to face the challenges ahead of him, where he is greeted by the entire town, who has gathered together to help their friend.

COMING ATTRACTIONS

The original theatrical trailer (what most of us call "coming attractions") for *It's a Wonderful Life* is a quaint example of the way Hollywood used to promote its big films. "Wonderful News about Wonderful People in a Wonderful Picture!" large letters proclaim. Then we hear the familiar strains of "Buffalo Gals" as the cast is shown, from Jimmy Stewart right on down to Frank Faylen (Ernie), Ward Bond (Bert), and Gloria Grahame (Violet). "Never before," says a somewhat bombastic announcer, "has any film contained such a full measure of the joy of living." To prove its point, the scene in which Mary and George land in the swimming pool is shown. The trailer is also interesting for hawking the movie's love scenes, showing a scene between George and Mary *and* George and Violet. Seems like they were trying to add a little spice to George's life while gently deceiving the large audience they no doubt hoped to attract.

WHAT A TALENTED CAST!

It's a Wonderful Life is like the starving artist who goes unappreciated in his lifetime and becomes world-famous immediately after his death. It may have come up empty-handed at Oscar time, but the cream always rises to the top, and *It's a Wonderful Life* is full of plenty of cream. Five of the actors in *It's a Wonderful Life* won Oscars for other roles: Jimmy Stewart, best actor for The *Philadelphia Story* (1940); Donna Reed, best supporting actress for *From Here to Eternity* (1953); Lionel Barrymore, best actor in *A Free Soul* (1930/31); Thomas Mitchell, best supporting actor for *Stagecoach* (1939); and Gloria Grahame, best supporting actress for *The Bad and the Beautiful* (1952). Incidentally, director Frank Capra didn't fare too badly, either. He won three Oscars for Best Direction: *It Happened One Night* (1934), *Mr. Deeds Goes to Town* (1936), and *You Can't Take It with You* (1938).

WHAT THE CRITICS SAID

In *Variety*:
"The recounting of this life is just about flawless in its tender and natural treatment; only possible thin carping could be that the ending is slightly overlong and a shade too cloying for all tastes. . . . Donna Reed reaches full-fledged stardom. Lionel Barrymore lends a lot of lustre. Thomas Mitchell especially is effective as the lead's drunken uncle."

In the *New York Times*:
"A turkey dinner, with Christmas trimmings, is precisely what's cooking at the end of this quaint and engaging modern parable on virtue being its own reward. . . . As the hero, Mr. Stewart does a warmly appealing job, indicating that he has grown in stature as well as in talent during the years he was in the war. And Donna Reed is remarkably poised and gracious as his adoring sweetheart and wife. The weakness of the picture . . . is the sentimentality--its illusory concept of life."

BEHIND THE SCENES WITH *IT'S A WONDERFUL LIFE*

Jimmy Stewart was the only actor Frank Capra ever considered for the role of George Bailey, though under an earlier production team (who obviously didn't make the film), Cary Grant was to play George Bailey.

The original idea for *It's a Wonderful Life* came from a short story by Philip Van Doren Stern called "The Greatest Gift." In that story, the main character's name is George Knapp. For some reason, Hollywood decided that George Bailey had a better ring to it.

Most of *It's a Wonderful Life* was shot during the summer. The *It's a Wonderful Life* picnic, held on August 4, 1946, celebrated the completion of filming. Cast and crew were invited to enjoy a fun-filled day at Lake Malibu.

At the picnic, the cast of 370 people posed for a group picture. The photo was so large the camera had to pan from left to right. Jimmy Stewart and Frank Capra appeared on both sides of the still photo. They had to run behind everyone to the other side of the photo while the camera was panning.

More than 3,000 tons of ice were used to create all the snow scenes in the movie--not one flake of snow was real, since the entire film was shot on a set, rather than location.

In the *It's a Wonderful Life Book,* author Jeanine Basinger lists some of the surprising actors Frank Capra suggested for various roles. Among the names: Olivia De Havilland and Jean Arthur as Mary, Thomas

Mitchell (eventually cast as Uncle Billy) as the scheming Mr. Potter, Barry Fitzgerald and Frank Morgan (also known as the *Wizard of Oz*) as Uncle Billy, and Reginald Owen (of the 1938 version of *A Christmas Carol*) as Old Man Gower, the drugstore owner.

Veteran character actor Henry Travers, who would eventually lend his cherubic countenance to the role of Clarence the Angel, was originally considered by Capra for the roles of Uncle Billy and Peter Bailey (George's father)--but not for the role of Clarence!

Of actor Samuel S. Hinds, who played George's father, Peter Bailey, Capra once wrote: "He looks like a father. He's so perfect, he looks like two fathers."

In 1947, the year the film was released, Donna Reed and Jimmy Stewart also starred in a successful radio version of the story.

Frank Capra was born in Sicily in 1897 and immigrated to the United States when he was six years old. Throughout his life, he maintained his optimistic view of the United States as "the land of opportunity."

In conjunction with a promotion for Target Stores (which produced a line of miniature houses based on buildings in the movie), the *It's a Wonderful Life* kids (now all adults) toured the United States in the 1990s. One of their stops: the Hollywood Christmas Parade, in which they appeared on the Bedford Falls float. More than 750,000 fans lined the streets to cheer the remaining stars from their favorite movie.

The infamous swimming pool under the gym floor, into which George and Mary take an inelegant dip, was no special effects achievement. The scene was actually filmed at Beverly Hills High School, where such a high-tech gymnasium existed in 1946.

On the day Frank Capra began shooting the big Christmas Eve snow storm, the temperature on the set was a steamy 90 degrees Fahrenheit. No wonder George looked so tired running down the street wishing Bedford Falls a Merry Christmas.

Sheldon Leonard once said that the main reason he took the role of Nick the bartender was for the money. He wanted to buy Dodgers tickets!

Frank Capra hired a marksman to shoot the window out for Donna Reed in the scene where she and Jimmy Stewart throw rocks at the house. However, her first throw nailed a window and neatly shattered it, and the marksman was told to go home.

George falls into the water three times in *It's a Wonderful Life*: the first time when he saves his brother, Harry, from drowning, the second time when he and Mary fall into the high school pool, and the last time when he saves Clarence from drowning. Naturally, critics have had great fun interpreting these watery journeys as metaphors for birth and life.

The main street used in the film was one of the most extensive (and expensive) sets built in Hollywood up to that time. It was 300 yards long (that's three football fields) and made up of more than 70 storefront buildings. It also featured 20 transplanted oak trees.

Jimmy Stewart was so moved by the scene in which George prays to God in Mr. Martini's bar that he began weeping. Frank Capra, naturally, loved the touch, but as he had not been filming the scene in close-up, he asked Stewart to do the scene again, weeping, so that he could move the camera closer. Stewart was unable to replicate those sincere tears, so Capra and his technicians painstakingly blew up the original scene frame by frame without any loss of clarity or quality.

When Clarence takes George to the cemetery to see what happened to

Director Frank Capra had to tone down the telephone scene between (Kingsley)
Donna Reed and James Stewart when censors pronounced it too
passionate.

15

Harry, the name on the tombstone is clearly visible, yet the second time, the name is obscured by snow. In addition, Harry's years are listed as 1911-1919, which means he was eight when he died, not nine as Clarence states.

An early draft of the script had Clarence actually confronting Potter for the way he's persecuted George for so many years.

Uncle Billy's raven was actually Frank Capra's raven. He appeared in nearly every Capra picture.

Remember the scene in which Uncle Billy leaves the Bailey house after celebrating Harry's wedding? As he walks away from George, we hear him singing "My Wild Irish Rose," followed by the sound of falling trash cans. According to the *It's a Wonderful Life Book*, the sound effect was the result of a technician who had dozed off and inadvertently knocked over some props. Needless to say, it was the perfect touch and in tune with the character of Uncle Billy. Frank Capra was so pleased that he gave the technician a bonus.

If you own an original lobby poster of *It's a Wonderful Life*, consider yourself lucky. It now sells for about $2,000.

The famous telephone kissing scene between George and Mary (while a no-doubt bewildered Sam Wainwright listens in from New York) was so perfect the first time that Capra did only one take. Too bad. Jimmy Stewart and Donna Reed (both single at the time) really seem to be enjoying themselves.

When Sam Wainwright comes to visit George and Mary as they're helping the Martinis move into their new house in Bailey Park, the pretty woman with him is not supposed to be just another girlfriend, but rather, his wife. (The script lists her name as Jane.) She was played by Marian Carr.

The fictional town of Bedford Falls is located in New York State. Some of the towns surrounding Bedford Falls have rather odd names: Aspetuck, Kitchawan, Katonah, and Chappaqua.

According to Frank Capra, the most difficult scene to shoot was the scene in which George Bailey comes home, defeated and depressed after Uncle Billy has lost $8,000. Capra said that it was difficult to balance George's uncharacteristic aggression toward his children with the more comical elements of the scene, such as Janie playing "Hark! The Herald Angels Sing!" on the piano ("Janie, haven't you learned that silly tune yet?" George snaps) and little Tommy saying, "Excuse me, excuse me . . . I burped!"

The scene in which Geoge Bailey gives his honeymoon money away to the Building & Loan customers provided a bit of spontaneity. Capra had a young Ellen Corby come up to the window and ask George for an unusual amount--$17.50. Stewart wasn't told how much she would be requesting and was so surprised by the modest request that, staying in character, he leaned across the counter and kissed Corby gratefully, adding a memorable moment to the scene.

If Beulah Bondi and Jimmy Stewart seem to have some genuine mother-and-son chemistry, it's no surprise. Bondi played Stewart's mother in seven films.

Jimmy Stewart was a Princeton University graduate who majored in architecture, something George Bailey would have appreciated.

In the film, the character George Bailey was born in 1907, which means that when the film ends in 1945, he is supposed to be 38. In real life, Jimmy Stewart was also 38 when he made the film. Donna Reed, incidentally, was a very young 25.

Frank Capra was a stickler for detail. He had his staff check on what the weather had been like in New York State on the day of the run on the banks in 1933. When he discovered it was raining, he worked that into the film, giving George and Mary a very wet wedding day.

Mr. Gower the druggist was played by the British character actor H. B. Warner. At the time *It's a Wonderful Life* was made, his most famous role was probably that of Jesus Christ in Cecil B. DeMille's 1927 film *King of Kings.*

If you think that Ernie the taxi driver looks familiar, check your television memory. Actor Frank Faylen played Dobie Gillis' dad in that popular sitcom.

Frank Capra made no secret of the fact that *It's a Wonderful Life* was his favorite film. He showed it in his home every Christmas Eve.

One of the best scenes in the movie is when Mary and George talk on the phone together to Sam Wainwright in New York. It's been listed by many fans and critics as one of the most romantic love scenes ever. It turns out it could have been even more romantic. The original version was so passionate that the Hollywood censors had Capra tone it down.

TRIVIA QUIZZES

MEET OUR HERO

George Bailey is one of the most memorable characters to ever emerge from Hollywood, thanks to a wonderful script and Jimmy Stewart's great performance. How much do you know about George?

1. What is George building in his living room?
2. What does George prevent Mr. Gower from doing?
3. What does George say are the three most exciting sounds in the world?

4. According to Mr. Potter, it's all over town that George has been giving money to whom?
5. What does Sam Wainwright say that George is always doing?
6. At Martini's, what kind of man does George say he *isn't?*
7. How does George save Harry's life?
8. Why was George rejected by the draft board when he tried to enlist?

ANSWERS: 1. A model of a bridge. 2. Accidentally sending poisoned pills to a customer. 3. Train whistles, plane engines, and anchor chains. 4. Violet. 5. Making a speech. 6. A praying man. 7. Prevents him from falling through the ice. 8. He was 4F due to his bad ear.

HOW WONDERFUL WAS GEORGE'S LIFE?

We all know that George Bailey changed the lives of almost everyone he came in contact with. Explain exactly how these characters' lives would have gone if there had been no George Bailey.

1. Uncle Billy
2. Mary
3. George's mother
4. Ernie
5. Mr. Gower
6. Harry Bailey
7. Violet

ANSWERS: 1. Uncle Billy winds up in an insane asylum after losing his business. 2. Mary remains a spinster. 3. George's mother becomes the embittered proprietor of "Ma Bailey's Boarding House." 4. Ernie lives in a shack in Potter's Field, deserted by his wife and child. 5. Mr. Gower, after serving time for poisoning a little boy, is a homeless wino. 6. Harry Bailey drowned at the age of eight. 7. Violet is a prostitute.

WHAT HAPPENED NEXT?

With its flashbacks and glimpses at what might have have been, the plot of It's a Wonderful Life *is pretty complicated. Which scenes follow which?*

1. George and Uncle Billy meet Harry at the station
2. George smashes his car into a tree.
3. George turns down a job from Potter.
4. Harry Bailey gets ready for the big dance.
5. George and Mary talk to Sam on the telephone.
6. George gives his own money away to shareholders.

A. George goes home to Mary at the Old Granville House.
B. George and Mary dance the Charleston.
C. George and Mary get married and leave in Ernie's cab.
D. Mary tells George that she is pregnant.
E. Mrs. Bailey throws a big party.
F. George contemplates suicide.

ANSWERS: 1-E, 2-F, 3-D, 4-B, 5-C, 6-A.

BEARING GIFTS, WE TRAVERSE TO GEORGE

At the very end of the movie, George's friends gather to help him out of his financial crisis. What did each of these characters bring (or send)?

1. Mr. Martini
2. Annie
3. Violet
4. Sam Wainwright
5. Harry Bailey

ANSWERS: 1. Mr. Martini brings cash after raiding the "juka-boxa." 2. Annie bring the money she's been saving for a divorce "if ever I get a husband." 3. Mr. Gower makes a raid on his charge accounts. 4. Violet decides not to leave town, thus returning George's money. 5. Sam Wainwright cables that his office can advance George "up to $25,000." 6. Harry Bailey offers a heartfelt toast, "To my big brother, George--the richest man in town."

IN A WORD

What is the significance of each of these words?

1. Tom Sawyer
2. Cigar lighter
3. Roasted chicken
4. National Geographic
5. $2,000
6. Congressional Medal of Honor
7. Burp
8. Football uniform

ANSWERS: 1. Tom Sawyer *is the novel Clarence is reading. 2. George always makes a wish on the cigar lighter in Mr. Gower's store. 3. Mary prepares roasted chicken on her and George's wedding night. 4. As a boy, George subscribes to* National Geographic. *5. George and Mary's honeymoon fund. 6. Harry Bailey wins the Congressional Medal of Honor. 7. George's youngest son, Tommy, follows George around the house saying, "Excuse me" because he burped. 8. After George and Mary fall in the pool, George wears a football uniform in place of his soggy suit.*

WHO SAID IT?

Match these memorable lines of dialogue to the characters who said them.

1.	"George Bailey, I'll love you till the day I die."	A. Mr. Potter
2.	"I changed my mind, George. I'm not going."	B. Mary
3.	"Looks like she can keep Harry on his toes."	C. Violet
4.	"Harry's a genius at research."	D. George
5.	"Hey! We must be pretty good!"	E. Ruth
6.	"You used to be so cocky!"	F. Harry
7.	"I'm chairman of the eats committee."	G. Ma Bailey

ANSWERS: 1-B, 2-C, 3-G, 4-E, 5-D, 6-A, 7-F.

MUSICAL INTERLUDES

You may not realize it, but music played an important role in It's a

Wonderful Life. *Can you identify the significance of these musical selections in the plot of* It's a Wonderful Life?

1. "I Love You Truly"
2. "Auld Lang Syne"
3. "Hark! The Herald Angels Sing!"
4. "Buffalo Gals"

ANSWERS: 1. On George and Mary's wedding night, Bert and Ernie sere-nade them with an off-key rendition of "I Love You Truly." 2. This, of course, is the song everyone gathers to sing in the movie's final scene. 3. Janie Bailey plays this song "over and over" on the piano, much to a frazzled George's distress. It's also sung at the party at the end of the movie. 4. If you're reading this book, you must know this one. George and Mary dance to this tune at the graduation dance and sing it on the way home, carrying their wet clothes. It becomes "their song." It also provides the music for the opening and closing credits.

MINOR PLAYERS

Sure, you know the name of George Bailey's wife. (Who doesn't?) But how many of these minor players can you match to a description of their role in the movie?

1.	Marty	A.	The Bailey family maid
2.	Bert	B.	George's childhood employer
3.	Mrs. Hatch	C.	Mary's brother
4.	Mr. Gower	D.	Harry Bailey's wife
5.	Ernie	E.	The town cabby
6.	Joseph	F.	The town police officer
7.	Violet	G.	Clarence the angel's boss
8.	Annie	H.	George's oldest daughter
9.	Ruth	I.	Mary's mother
10.	Janie	J.	The town hussy

ANSWERS: 1-C, 2-F, 3-I, 4-B, 5-E, 6-G, 7-J, 8-A, 9-D, 10-H.

CHARACTER ACTORS

1. Gloria Grahame, who played Violet Bick, played another woman of flexible morals in a movie version of a Rodgers and Hammerstein musical. Name it.
2. Lionel Barrymore was known for his annual radio performances of what famous Christmas tale?
3. Where else will you find two buddies named Bert and Ernie?
4. What *Our Gang* star plays Mary's date at the dance?
5. Sheldon Leonard, Nick the bartender, later became a well-known television producer. What classic comedy about a television writer did he produce?
6. Thomas Mitchell (Uncle Billy) played the father of one of the screen's most famous heroines. Name her.

ANSWERS: 1. She played Ado Annie in Oklahoma. *2.* A Christmas Carol. *3. On* Sesame Street. *4. Carl "Alfalfa" Switzer. 5.* The Dick Van Dyke Show. *6. Scarlett O'Hara in* Gone with the Wind.

BITS & PIECES

1. What studio released *It's a Wonderful Life*?
2. What was the name of the 1977 television remake?
3. What was unusual about the leading role in that remake?
4. Who received first billing in *It's a Wonderful Life*?
5. What is the last line in the movie?
6. What is Zuzu a nickname for?
7. In what categories was *It's a Wonderful Life* nominated for Oscars?
8. What movie won Best Picture that year?
9. What actor won the Oscar over Jimmy Stewart?
10. What director won the Oscar over Frank Capra?

ANSWERS: 1. RKO/Liberty. 2. It Happened One Christmas. 3. The leading role became Mary Hatch, as played by Marlo Thomas. 4. Jimmy Stewart, of course. 5. "Atta boy, Clarence!" 6. We aren't told. 7. Best Picture, Best Actor, Best Director, Sound Recording, and Film Editing. 8. The Best Years of Our Lives. *9. Fredric March for* The Best Years of Our Lives. *10. William Wyler for* The Best Years of Our Lives--*see a pattern forming?*

WHITE CHRISTMAS

VITAL STATISTICS

Year Released: 1954
Studio: Paramount

Director: Michael Curtiz
Writers: Norman Krasna, Norman Panama, and Melvin Frank
Cast: Bing Crosby, Danny Kaye, Rosemary Clooney, Vera-Ellen,
     Dean Jagger, and Mary Wickes

Academy Award Nominations: 1
Academy Awards Won: 0

Claim to Fame: Probably the only movie ever created to capitalize on the vast popularity of a contemporary song. For many of us, this was our first introduction to Irving Berlin's classic ode to snow. It also made Rosemary Clooney, a velvet-voiced singer who made only a handful of films, a household name. Though over the years *White Christmas* has earned more than its share of critical drubbings, the public doesn't seem to care. Video and DVD sales are strong, and it is televised in almost every major city each Christmas season. The bottom line is, people find the movie both warm and entertaining. Besides, think of all those little girls who have performed their version of "Sisters" to adoring parents--you just can't buy that kind of movie magic!

THE STORY

Two old army buddies, Broadway producers Bob Wallace and Phil Davis (Bing Crosby and Danny Kaye), find themselves with time on their hands and girls on their minds one Christmas. The girls, Betty and Judy Haynes (Rosemary Clooney and Vera-Ellen), are a clean-scrubbed song-and-dance team booked for the holidays at an inn in Vermont, and Bob and Phil join them. When the gang arrives in Vermont, three surprises await them: there is no snow; the inn doesn't need Betty and Judy's act due to a lack of guests, and the owner of the inn is none other than Bob and Phil's old commanding officer, General Tom Waverly (Dean Jagger). The foursome does what it can to help the inn's slow business by putting together a "really dynamite" act. But Bob, ever intuitive, knows that's not enough--General Waverly misses being a general. A few misunderstandings occur before all the loose ends are tied up, but then true love wins, the General is happy again, and the entire casts sings "White Christmas."

WHAT THE CRITICS SAID

In *Variety*:
"The directional handling by Michael Curtiz gives a smooth blend of music . . . and drama, and in the climax creates a genuine heart tug that will squeeze tears. . . . Crosby wraps up his portion of the show with deceptive ease."

In the *New York Times*:
"The notion of starring Mr. Crosby in a film that would have the title 'White Christmas,' was broached as long as six years ago. . . . But, oddly enough, the confection is not so tasty as one might support [sic]. Everyone works hard at the business of singing, dancing and cracking jokes, but the stuff that they work with is minor. . . . The credited screenwriters . . . have shown very little imagination in putting togeth-

er what is sometimes called the 'book.' Three numbers are given over to the admiration of general and Army life."

THE SEARCH FOR A COSTAR

The role of Phil Davis was originally written for Fred Astaire. He seemed a natural choice--after all, he and Bing had starred in two previous Irving Berlin films: *Holiday Inn* and *Blue Skies*. There are still remnants of Fred's spirit in the movie--that long dance sequence, "The Best Things Happen When You're Dancing," was clearly conceived with a dancer in mind. But for reasons known only to Astaire, he turned down the role. The producers then turned to Donald O'Connor, who had recently been a sensation in *Singin' in the Rain*. O'Connor, however, pleaded injury and also had to turn down the role. Finally, someone thought of Danny Kaye, not really known as a musical star (though we think he did a fine job of dancing). He asked for a few changes in the script (which led to more than a few criticisms of the choppy storyline) and then agreed to take on the role. The rest is history, and whether or not Kaye considered it a good role, *White Christmas* certainly helped to make him a recognizable name to several generations.

DON'T CALL IT A REMAKE

For some reason, many people persist in referring to *White Christmas* as a remake of or a sequel to *Holiday Inn*. Wrong! Anyone who says that clearly hasn't watched either movie in quite a while. Still, there are some similarities: the male entertaining teams (though in *White Christmas*, Bing Crosby's character is a workaholic, as opposed to the lazy Jim in *Holiday Inn*), the New England settings (Vermont in this picture; Connecticut in the other), the charming inns, and, finally, the lovely female costars. There 's even a sense of déjà vu in the final musical segment. In *Holiday Inn*, Virginia Dale unexpectedly joins the final song-and-dance number, and in *White Christmas*, Rosemary Clooney surprises Bing Crosby by returning to the act. For the record, Rosemary Clooney herself, in her 2001 autobiography *Girl Singer*, calls *White Christmas* a "partial remake" of *Holiday Inn*--come to think of it, maybe that *is* a good description!

BEHIND THE SCENES WITH WHITE CHRISTMAS

Clooney said it was Crosby himself who suggested her as his co-star in *White Christmas*. In the summer of 1951, Crosby wrote a letter to Paramount producers stating, "How about a dame called Rosemary Clooney? Sings a good song--and is purportedly personable." Three years later, Crosby's suggestion became a reality.

Once Clooney and Crosby met, they became good friends. They often sang together on radio and television specials and enjoyed watching prize fights together on TV. He even wrote the introduction to her 1977 autobiography, *This for Remembrance* (her second autobiography *Girl Singer*, was published in 2001).

Clooney said that the reason she and Crosby sounded so well together was that they had virtually the same singing range. "Mine was an octave and five notes, while Bing's was probably larger, but at least that. . . . We didn't have to make concessions to accommodate our voices."

Vera-Ellen was involved in another Christmas classic, of sorts. Early in her career, she had been a high-steppin' Rockette and had appeared in their Christmas shows in New York City.

Bing Crosby met his second wife, Kathryn Grant (real name, Olive Grandstaff), on the set of *White Christmas*. She was 30 years younger than him and was rushing past his dressing room returning some costumes to the wardrobe mistress when she tripped and fell. Crosby invited her into his dressing room to catch her breath. Only a few weeks before, she had tried out for the role of young Susan, the General's granddaughter in *White Christmas*, but had failed to get the part. A few days after their meeting, Crosby invited the young actress to visit the *White Christmas* set with a friend, and he even pulled up a chair for her while she watched.

The hilarious scene in which Crosby and Kaye lip-synch the song "Sisters" was arrived at only after a bit of compromise. Originally, they were to have worn blue dresses in the scene, but Crosby refused to appear "in drag." Clever costume designer Edith Head quickly came up with a compromise and had the two male stars simply roll up their pant legs, put on headdresses, and carry feathered fans. Maybe Crosby's fears were justified. Apparently, the producers of the film got a letter from the Legion of Decency warning them that nothing should "lend a flavor of a 'pansy' routine to this bit of business."

In the final sequence, General Waverly blows out all the candles on his cake. By the very end of the movie, the candles are lit again.

When Bob visits Phil in the army hospital, he's takes a seat at the end of Phil's bed. In the very next shot, he's sitting next to Phil without having moved at all.

The same male dancers surround Betty at the Columbia Inn *and* at the Carousel Club!

Even in the 1950s, when the film was made, Irving Berlin was carefully watching over his pet song, "White Christmas." He was on the set when Crosby sang the song to the troops in the film's opening and was still giving him suggestions on how it should be sung.

White Christmas proved a big moneymaker for Irving Berlin. In addition to being paid $300,000 for the rights to his songs, he also got 30 percent of the film's profits (in its initial release, the film grossed $12 million). Bing Crosby and Paramount Pictures also got 30 percent each of the profits, with the remaining 10 percent going to Danny Kaye. Rosemary Clooney and Vera-Ellen had to settle for salaries. According to Clooney, she was paid $5,000 a week for her work in the movie, which was double the salary she had received for her few previous motion pictures.

As Bob and Phil run to catch the train to New York, a conductor can be

In a moment reminiscent of Holiday Inn's *final scene, Rosemary* (Kingsley) *Clooney re-joins the foursome in* White Christmas.

seen inside the train hurrying to help them aboaard. In the next shot, they're already on the train, and the conductor is approaching them at a leisurely pace.

Once Bob and Phil make it to the club car, they bring their luggage with them, with Bob actually setting his in the aisle next to the booth. A few minutes later the girls come in, and the luggage has disappeared.

The film has often been criticized for its less-than-tight plot. (Why does Betty get mad at Bob but not Phil? When does Emma realize she was wrong about Bob and Phil's television plans?) In fact, the writers were brought in *after* the stars had been signed and some of the sets had been built (the writers were given a rough idea of what the story was supposed to be about). Film buffs also noticed some plot similarities in *White Christmas* and another film directed by Michael Curtiz, *I'll See You in My Dreams*--though that film had different writers.

White Christmas was the first movie to be filmed in the widescreen technique known as VistaVision, Paramount's answer to 20th-Century Fox's CinemaScope. Using this technique, the film is run through the camera horizontally rather than vertically.

When Edith Head sat down to design Rosemary's Clooney's clothes for *White Christmas*, she already knew the star pretty well. She had designed the suit Clooney wore for her July 1953 marriage to Jose Ferrer. When it came time to make *White Christmas*, the anxious new-lywed was hoping it would wrap up quickly so that she could be with her new husband.

Although Rosemary Clooney played the big sister and "mother hen" to Vera-Ellen, their actual ages tell a different story. Vera-Ellen was 34, Clooney 26, when the movie was made.

White Christmas marked the end of Vera-Ellen's (real name, Vera Ellen

Rohe) American film career. She only made one more film after it, the British movie *Let's Be Happy*, before retiring from films. She died in 1981.

Dean Jagger, who played General Tom Waverly, was reportedly unhappy with his role in *White Christmas*, in part because he had to wear a toupee for the role.

In *This for Remembrance*, Clooney recounts how hard she had to work on the simple steps for the "Sisters" number, especially when she was working with a dancer as talented as Vera-Ellen. (According to Clooney, she didn't even like ballroom dancing.) Clooney had come to films strictly on her talent as a singer and more specifically on the merits of her big hit, "Come on-a My House." Her mentor as a singer had been Mitch Miller.

The cast and crew of *White Christmas* were forced to perform the big "White Christmas" finale twice--all but Bing Crosby, that is. Once filming on the number was complete, director Curtiz was informed that the King and Queen of Greece were visiting Paramount and wanted to visit the set of the new Bing Crosby film. Curtiz asked everyone to report to the set that afternoon so they could perform the whole scene again--this time, however, there would be no film in the camera. Crosby, unimpressed by royalty and knowing that they had gotten the scene right the first time, refused to return. So that afternoon, while Clooney, Kaye, and Vera-Ellen twirled, danced, and looked happy, Crosby was noticeably absent, except on the prerecorded soundtrack. Clooney said she was pretty sure that the king and queen noticed his absence--especially since they could hear his characteristic mellow voice reverberating through the soundstage--but they were too polite to comment.

In a brief 1994 interview in *TV Guide*, Clooney recalled the making of *White Christmas* as a happy experience and said that it seemed like only yesterday that she had made the movie. She also said, with a refreshing lack of modesty, that when she saw herself in the film, she thought she looked "pretty cute."

In *Girl Singer*, Clooney recalls an amusing anecdote about eating on film. In one scene, the four lead players are sitting at the table in the lodge with bowls of soup in front of them. The scene was shot several ways, from a master shot to close-ups of the four actors. By the end of the session, Clooney threw her spoon down in frustration and said, "I can't eat anymore!" Only then did she notice that the soup bowls of her three costars were still full. "You're supposed to play with it, not eat it all!" Crosby teased good-naturedly.

TRIVIA QUIZZES

THE HAYNES SISTERS

Betty and Judy Haynes provide the movie with plenty of singing and dancing and help the plot to move along, too. But doesn't it seem to you that they get serious about their fellas very quickly?

1. How many times do we hear that catchy tune, "Sisters"?
2. What color eyes do each of the sisters have?
3. Who played Judy Haynes? Who played Betty Haynes?
4. What do Phil and Bob call Betty and Judy's brother?
5. How does Judy characterize Betty's behavior toward her?
6. What does Betty give Bob for Christmas?
7. What is the name of the nightclub Betty defects to?
8. What do Betty and Judy carry during the "Sisters" act?
9. What song do Phil and Judy dance to twice?

ANSWERS: 1. Three. 2. Betty has blue eyes; Judy, brown. 3. Vera-Ellen played Judy; Rosemary Clooney, Betty. 4. "Freckle-faced Haynes, the dog-faced boy." 5. Like a mother hen. 6. A figurine of a knight on a horse. 7. The Carousel Club. 8. Large blue-feathered fans. 9. "The Best Things Happen

When You're Dancing."

WHAT DO YOU DO WITH A GENERAL?

If it weren't for soft-spoken General Tom Waverly, we wouldn't have a story at all. Thanks to him, we get to see all those great song-and-dance numbers and we get our white christmas, too.

1. With what song do General Waverly's men salute him on his last night in command?
2. What does Phil mistake the General for when he sees him at the inn?
3. When the General tries to get back in the Army, what kind of job does he tell Bob he won't settle for?
4. What is the name of the General's granddaughter?
5. True of false--the General has sunk his life savings into the inn?
6. What is the name of the inn? In what Vermont town is it located?
7. Why does the General wear his uniform on the night of the big show?

ANSWERS: 1. "We'll Follow the Old Man" 2. A janitor. 3. A desk job. 4. Susan. 5. True. 6. Columbia Inn, Pine Tree, Vermont. 7. Because his housekeeper, Emma, has sent his other suits to the dry cleaners.

ALL SINGING, ALL DANCING

Match these Irving Berlin tunes with the characters who sang them. (Note: some songs will have more than one answer.)

1.	"Count Your Blessings"	A.	Phil
2.	"What Do You Do with a General?"	B.	Bob
3.	"Snow"	C.	Betty
4.	"Mandy"	D.	Judy
5.	"Choreography"	E.	Chorus
6.	"White Christmas"		
7.	"I Wish I Was Back in the Army"		
8.	"The Best Things Happen When You're Dancing"		

ANSWERS: 1-B, C. 2-B. 3-A, B, C, D. 4-A, B, C, E. 5-A. 6-A, B, C, D, E. 7-A, B, C, D. 8-A, E.

WITH A SONG IN THEIR HEARTS

Not too many great songwriters also write their own lyrics, but Irving Berlin is an exception. Let's see if you really listen when the gang starts singing these great songs.

1. In "Count Your Blessings," what does Bob think of when his bankroll gets small?
2. In the song "Snow," what does Judy want to wash in snow?
3. The song "Sisters" refers to the arrival of a "certain gentleman" from which European city?
4. In "The Best Things Happen When You're Dancing," what kind of guy comes out alright "if the girl is sweet"?
5. What kind of generals does Bob describe in the very last line of "What Do You Do with a General"?
6. In the song "We'll Follow the Old Man" why do we follow the old man?

ANSWERS: 1. "I think of when I had none at all." 2. Her hair. 3. Rome. 4. "Even guys with two left feet." 5. Unemployed. 6. "Because we love him."

WHAT HAPPENED NEXT?

For this matching quiz, take a plot element from the first column and match it with the plot element from the second column that immediately follows it in the movie.

1. Betty and Judy sneak out of their dressing room.

2. Betty has trouble sleeping.

3. Betty refuses to dance with Bob at the big party.

4. Bob and Phil argue about working too much.

A. Judy and Phil concoct their phony engagement scheme.

B. Bob visits Phil in his sick bed.

C. Bob sings "Count Your Blessings.

D. Bob and Phil meet Betty and Judy for the first time.

5. Bob saves Phil's life.

6. Bob and Betty fight about the "Blessings" numbe.r

7. General Waverly drives Betty to the station.

E. Bob and Phil lip-synch to "Sisters."

F. Judy and Phil announce their "engagement."

G. Judy receives a letter.

ANSWERS: 1-E, 2-C, 3-F, 4-D, 5-B, 6-A, 7-G.

WHO SAID IT?

Match the line of dialogue with the character who said it.

1. "I'm starting to play a little trombone myself."
2. "I own this place."
3. "I'm not exactly repulsive, am I?"
4. "No, they're brown."
5. "I could just kiss you."
6. "I understand television has entered the picture."

A. Judy
B. Emma
C. Phil
D. Bob
E. General Waverly
F. Betty

ANSWERS: 1-D, 2-E, 3-A, 4-C, 5-B, 6-F.

THAT HOTHEAD BETTY!

She may have looked like a cool blonde, but let's fact it--as played by Rosemary Clooney, Betty Haynes is a hothead. Do you remember these outbursts?

1. When Bob and Betty first meet, they're getting along fine until Bob says something that offends Betty. What does he say?
2. When they're tucked into their room at the inn for the night, what advice of Judy's does Betty peevishly follow, just to make Judy happy?
3. Later, Betty foolishly believes Emma's inaccurate eavesdropping. Angry with Bob, what does she say she wouldn't want to interfere with?

4. At the cast party, Betty dances with Phil but refuses to dance with
       Bob. A few minutes later, she refuses to drink to Phil and Judy's
       happiness with Bob. What beverage does she rudely refuse?
5. When she goes to work at the Carousel Club, Bob's appearance
       flusters her. What does she tell the club manager she wants to do?
6. How many times does Betty turn down Bob for a date when he
       shows up at the club?

ANSWERS: 1. "So even little Judy has an angle." 2. To go to the lodge and have a snack. 3. "The plans of the great Wallace and Davis." 4. A glass of champagne. 5. Drop the torchy love song she's rehearsed and substitute another song. Betty suggests "Blue Skies." 6. Twice.

IN A WORD

What is the significance of these words to the plot of White Christmas?

1. Extension line
2. Phil's right arm
3. A knight in shining armor
4. Firewood
5. The New England Chapter of Busybodies Anonymous
6. Club car
7. Stain on the carpet
8. Horseshoes
9. Carousel horses
10. A liverwurst sandwich

ANSWERS: 1. How Emma eavesdrops. 2. What Phil points to when he wants his way. 3. The too-idealistic Betty is always hoping one of these will come along. 4. What General Waverly is carrying when Phil first sees him at the inn. 5. The fictional organization Emma says she belongs to. 6. Where Bob and Phil have to sleep after Phil gives their train tickets to the girls. 7. The girls' landlord in Florida says they've stained the carpet. 8. When General Waverly starts playing horseshoes, Bob knows he needs help. 9. What the nightclub Betty flees to is decorated with. 10. One of the sandwiches Bob offers Betty before crooning "Count Your Blessings."

MINOR PLAYERS

White Christmas has a small supporting cast, but they contribute some memorable moments. Can you remember a bit about these bit players?

1. What tasteless "angle" does television personality Ed Harrison want Bob to go for in talking about the General?
2. What method does the housekeeper Emma use to read telegrams other people receive?
3. Throughout the film, Phil and Bob are followed by an annoying blonde chorus girl. What is her stock response when introduced to people?
4. What is the name of the nightclub owner Betty works for briefly?
5. Betty sings her torch song, "Love, You Didn't Do Right by Me" surrounded by a group of young men. One of them went on to win an Academy Award for his performance in *West Side Story*. Can you name him?

ANSWERS: 1. Ed wants to go with the "forgotten man" angle, but Bob says no. 2. Emma steams them open, declaring that only amateurs hold them up to the light. 3. "Mutual, I'm sure." 4. Dick. 5. George Chakiris, who played Bernardo in West Side Story.

BITS AND PIECES

1. Which leg does Phil pretend to hurt?
2. Where does Betty tell Judy their brother is currently stationed?
3. What is the name of the musical Bob and Phil stage at the inn?
4. What does General Waverly whisper to Bob in the touching final scene?
5. How many kids does Phil wish Bob had?
6. For what classic, Academy Award-winning drama is director Michael Curtiz best known?
7. Who designed the costumes for *White Christmas?*
8. What studio released *White Christmas?*
9. Who got first billing in *White Christmas?*

ANSWERS: 1. Left. 2. Alaska. 3. Playing Around. *4. "I'm grateful, Captain." 5. Nine. 6.* Casablanca. *7. Eight-time Academy Award winner Edith Head. 8. Paramount. 9. Bing Crosby, of course!*

MIRACLE ON 34TH STREET

VITAL STATISTICS
Year Released: 1947
Studio: 20th-Century Fox

Director: George Seaton
Writer: George Seaton
Cast: Maureen O'Hara, Edmund Gwenn, Natalie Wood, John Payne, Gene Lockhart, William Frawley, and Thelma Ritter

Academy Award Nominations: 4
Academy Awards Won: 3

Claim to Fame: One of the few films that presents Santa Claus as a serious character, rather than one played for laughs. This film also made regional department store Macy's a familiar name from coast to coast, even in towns where there is no Macy's. Anyone who's seen this movie knows exactly what street Macy's is on, should they find themselves in New York City. This film also featured a fine juvenile performance by Natalie Wood. She is adorable in this film, and it's hard to believe that just eight years later she'd be playing a troubled teen in *Rebel without a Cause.*

THE STORY

It's Thanksgiving morning, and Doris Walker (Maureen O'Hara) is supervising the last-minute details of Macy's big parade. But she's dismayed to find that the parade's Santa Claus is drunk. Strangely enough, a little man (Edmund Gwenn) who looks just like Santa Claus is standing nearby. Can he stand in? she asks. He agrees to do so and is such a hit that he's subsequently hired by Macy's to play Santa Claus throughout the holiday season. The only trouble is, the old man insists he really *is* Santa Claus (he calls himself Kris Kringle). Doris is thrown into turmoil. Should she fire him? Mr. Macy, after all, seems to like him. And then there's Doris' daughter, Susan (Natalie Wood). She seems to believe in Kris, too. Things get more complicated when the store psychologist takes a strong dislike to Kris and drags him off to Bellevue, the mental hospital. Before we know it, Kris is on trial: is he really Santa Claus or isn't he? Leave it to hotshot attorney Fred Gailey (John Payne) to win the case--and Doris' heart, too.

WHAT THE CRITICS SAID

In *Variety*:
"Film is an actor's holiday. . . . Edmund Gwenn's Santa Claus performance proves the best of his career. Gene Lockhart's performance as the judge is a gem. Surprise moppet performance is turned in by Natalie Wood. . . . It's a standout, natural portrayal."

In the *New York Times*:
"Let us heartily recommend the Roxy's new picture, 'Miracle on 34th Street.' As a matter of fact, let's go further: let's catch its spirit and heartily proclaim that it is the freshest little picture in a long time, and maybe even the best comedy of the year. Edmund Gwenn . . . [plays] Kris Kringle with such natural and warm benevolence that, if ever the real Santa wants to step down, Mr. Gwenn is the man for the job."

AND THE WINNER IS . . . .

Hopes were running high on March 20, 1948--Oscar night. It was the Academy Award's twentieth birthday, and the stars came out to glitter. Would *Miracle on 34th Street* be the big winner? It was nominated in four categories, most of them big ones: Best Picture, Best Supporting Actor, Best Screenplay, and Original Story. In the Best Picture category it faced stiff competition from *Gentleman's Agreement*, a serious look at anti-Semitism, and--surprisingly--another Christmas film, *The Bishop's Wife*, which was nominated in five categories, including Best Director. Would *Miracle on 34th Street* be harmed by its relatively lightweight theme? Or had viewers forgotten it? After all, it had been released in June, long before the Academy members actually got their ballots. History tells us that *Miracle on 34th Street* wasn't the big winner, but it did quite well nonetheless. It managed to win three out of its four nominations, losing only Best Picture. Not too surprisingly, that went to *Gentleman's Agreement*. But it did fare better than its fellow Christmas nominee, *The Bishiop's Wife*, which won only for Sound Recording. Best of all, Edmund Gwenn won an Oscar for his portrayal of Kris Kringle, and his acceptance speech stayed in the spirit of the movie: "Now I know there's a Santa Claus."

A VALENTINE FOR CHRISTMAS

What came first, the movie or the book? In this case, the story came first, then the movie, then the book. Here's what happened: Valentine Davies was a well-known screenwriter in Hollywood. (In fact, he later served as president of both the Screenwriter's Guild and the Academy of Motion Picture Arts and Sciences, the organization that hands out the Oscars.) But back in the 1940s, he was more concerned with Christmas and, more particularly, the commercialization of it. Davies said that he conceived the plot of *Miracle on 34th Street* while waiting in line at a department store one December. This experience, combined with his annual viewing of the Macy's Thanksgiving Day Parade from the window of his New York apartment, combined to create the bones of the plot we know so well today. He shared his idea with his good friend, director George Seaton, who actually wrote the screenplay. On Oscar night both Davies and Seaton walked away with Oscars. After the Academy Awards, Davies was asked to flesh out the story of *Miracle on 34th Street* and turn it into a novel. He was happy to do so. Today, his novelization is still available in an illustrated edition for children.

BEHIND THE SCENES WITH MIRACLE ON 34TH STREET

Miracle on 34th Street was shot on location in New York City in 1946. This was unusual at a time when Hollywood excelled at building elaborate and realistic-looking sets. Director George Seaton even obtained permission from Macy's department store to shoot some scenes there, in order to get the appropriate holiday hustle-bustle.

When producer John Hughes made his 1994 version of *Miracle*, Macy's wasn't feeling so friendly. Not only did the powers that be not permit filming in the store, but they wouldn't even let the Macy's name be used (in the film, the store is called C. F. Coles). Gimbel's department store similarly refused Hughes permission to use its name.

According to the book *Best American Screenplays*, edited by Sam Thomas, George Seaton and Valentine Davies wrote themselves into a corner in the climactic courtroom scene and couldn't think of a way to end the film. Having U.S. postal employees carrying in the sacks of mail to "prove" that Kris is the one and only Santa Claus was a last-minute inspiration. In the John Hughes remake, the joyous mailbag sequence was eliminated entirely.

Director George Seaton became such good friends with Edmund Gwenn that he was by the actor's side when he died in a hospital in 1959. When Seaton commented that dying must be a very difficult thing, Gwenn commented, "Not as hard as playing comedy."

Two titles were originally suggested for the film: *My Heart Tells Me* and *The Big Heart*. No one knows who came up with the far-catchier title *Miracle on 34th Street*. In England, the film was released under the title *The Big Heart*.

The project was not a favorite of producer Darryl Zanuck, who wasn't sure it had much box-office appeal. He thought that in early drafts of

Maureen O'Hara and Edmund Gwenn got along famously on the (Kingsley) *set of* Miracle on the 34th Street. *O'Hara joked that she really believed he was Santa Claus.*

the script Maureen O'Hara's character was too hard. In subsequent drafts, Doris was softened up. Zanuck also alloted director Seaton a relatively meager budget, in addition to releasing the film in the summer of 1947, rather than risk having it bomb during the all-important holiday season. Zanuck was categorically proved wrong, and the film was still playing to packed houses in December 1947.

One thing Zanuck was high on was Maureen O'Hara. He was extremely impressed by her performance as Angharad in *How Green Was My Valley*, made when she was only 21. She was 26 when she made *Miracle*, and had starred mostly in costume dramas in-between the two films. *Miracle* gave her an opportunity to play a contemporary businesswoman, a challenge she relished.

Darryl Zanuck was known as one of Hollywood's strictest bosses. One of his most memorable quotations is, "Don't say yes until I finish talking." He had started out as a scriptwriter for the Rin-Tin-Tin films but by the time his career was complete, he had produced such classics as *The Grapes of Wrath, Gentleman's Agreement* (*Miracle's* Oscar competition), and *All About Eve*. His penchant for earnest dramas that made audiences "think" also resulted in a big bomb, *Wilson*, about the twenty-seventh U.S. president.

Low-key leading man John Payne had a varied career. His role in *Miracle* is probably his best known, but he also starred in lightweight musicals with Betty Grable and in the tense Somerset Maugham drama *The Razor's Edge*. In the 1950s, he starred in the TV western series *The Restless Gun*.

Maureen O'Hara's appeal always lay partly in her fiery Irish personality. But apparently, Hollywood didn't think she was Irish enough. Although her real name was Maureen Fitzsimons, they changed it to O'Hara. She was born in Dublin, Ireland, and been a member of Dublin's famed Abbey Players before making her way to Hollywood.

43

With her vivid red hair and green eyes, Maureen O'Hara had a nickname in Hollywood: the Queen of Technicolor. Another red-haired actress, Lucille Ball (who had blue eyes), was sometimes referred to as Tessie Technicolor.

Natalie Wood, whose real name was Natasha Gudrun (both of her parents were born in Russia), was the daughter of an ambitious Hollywood mother who wanted her beautiful daughter to be a star. Director Irving Pichel also thought the brown-eyed youngster had potential and gave her the last name of his good friend, director Sam Wood.

Fourteen cameras were used to shoot the actual Macy's Thanksgiving Day parade used in the film.

During the filming of *Miracle*, the film's production crew took over more than three floors at Macy's department store.

In addition to having a mother who spent a lot of time watching over her on the set, Natalie Wood had a father who worked at 20th-Century Fox in a variety of technical capacities. When her younger sister, Lana, tried to break into films, she, too, used the surname Wood.

Though the character of Susan Walker is supposed to be six years old, Natalie Wood was actually nine when she made the movie.

The District Attorney (whose name, incidentally, is Thomas Mara) was played by Jerome Cowan. He is best known for his performance as Miles Archer, Sam Spade's partner, in the Humphrey Bogart classic *The Maltese Falcon*.

Actress Thelma Ritter (who played the harassed shopper at Macy's) made her first film appearance in *Miracle on 34th Street*. She was to become one of Hollywood's most durable supporting actresses and was nominated for the Academy Award for best supporting actress a record

Though disappointed that she was called away from a quiet family (Kingsley)
Christmas in Ireland, Maureen O'Hara found the making of Miracle
on 34th Street *a delightful experience.*

six times: *All About Eve* (1950), *The Mating Season* (1951), *With a Song in My Heart* (1952), *Pickup on South Street* (1953), *Pillow Talk* (1959), and *The Birdman of Alcatraz* (1962). Unbelievably, she didn't win even once. She died in 1969.

Philip Tonge--whose character, Mr. Sawyer, spends a lot of time trying to please his boss, R. H. Macy--got to play the boss to teen idol Tab Hunter in the 1950s sitcom *The Tab Hunter Show*.

While shooting *Miracle*, Natalie Wood was also filming *The Ghost and Mrs. Muir* with Gene Tierney and Rex Harrison. For that film, she adopted an English accent.

Maureen O'Hara was in Ireland with her baby daughter, Bronwyn Bridget, when she learned that 20th-Century Fox wanted her for a Christmas movie. She was not thrilled, as it was her first trip back to Ireland since wartime travel restrictions had been lifted, and she had been home a mere two days. But like a good studio employee (with a seven-year contract!), she returned to the U.S. to find herself completely enchanted by the script.

Maureen O'Hara loved working with John Payne and once fondly observed that she made five movies with John Payne and five movies with John Wayne. She and Payne often went out for meals together, and Payne would tease her, saying, "You've got to smile more, Maureen! You look like you're mad at something!" To which the young actress would reply, "Well, maybe I am!"

Natalie Wood and Maureen O'Hara got along famously on the set, and little Natalie even dubbed her on-screen mother "Mama Maureen." Each day, she brought O'Hara little gifts she had made out of clay.

In a 1998 interview, Maureen O'Hara recalled how very cold it was when they shot the final scene on Long Island in which Susan sees her dream house. There were no elaborate mobile trailers in which the stars could shelter, and in between takes, everyone stood in the subzero temperature, stomping their feet to keep warm. O'Hara recalled, "The lady who lived across the street saw our problem and invited everyone into her house to warm up!" To show her appreciaiton, O'Hara took the woman out to lunch at the 21 Club in New York when filming was complete.

In the same interview, when asked whether she had seen any of the *Miracle on 34th Street* remakes, O'Hara responded with a spirited and curt, "No!"

TRIVIA QUIZZES

WHO'S WHO

Some of the studio system's finest character actors make up the cast of Miracle on 34th Street--*some in roles so small the characters don't even have names. What character did each of these actors play?*

1.	Natalie Wood	A.	A post office employee
2.	Jack Albertson	B.	Judge Henry X. Harper
3.	William Frawley	C.	Kris Kringle
4.	John Payne	D.	Charlie, the judge's adviser
5.	Maureen O'Hara	E.	Susan Walker
6.	Edmund Gwenn	F.	A harried holiday shopper
7.	Gene Lockhart	G.	Doris Walker
8.	Thelma Ritter	H.	Fred Gailey
9.	Porter Hall	I.	Mr. Sawyer

ANSWERS: 1-E, 2-A, 3-D, 4-H, 5-G, 6-C, 7-B, 8-F, 9-I.

BITS & PIECES

Here are some general questions for the truly observant.

1. What studio released the movie?
2. What traditional carol is peppered throughout the movie's soundtrack?
3. How does the movie open? What is unusual about the way it is shot?
4. Other than Gimbel's, to what other famous New York department store does Macy's send its customers?
5. On what floor of Macy's do children go to see Santa Claus?
6. What is the starting time for the parade?
7. What is the newspaper ad's guarantee about the parade?
8. How old is Alfred, Kris' young friend at Macy's?
9. The one and only time we see Doris' maid, Cleo, what is she doing?
10. What storeowner, other than R. H. Macy, is portrayed in the movie?

ANSWERS: 1. Twentieth-Century Fox. 2. "Jingle Bells" 3. Kris Kringle walking down the street. It is shot as though we are following him. 4. Bloomingdale's. 5. Seventh. 6. 10:00 a.m. 7. "Rain or shine." 8. Seventeen. 9. Stuffing a turkey. 10. Mr. Gimbel.

IS HE REALLY SANTA CLAUS?

Here they are: five clues that make us think Kris is the real thing.

1. At the beginning of the film, Kris points out three mistakes in a window display of Santa's reindeers. What are they?
2. What does Kris show Macy's drunken Santa Claus how to do correctly?
3. Susan likes the fact that Kris doesn't wear glasses. What else about his appearance does she find convincing?
4. Susan also observes Kris making friends with a little girl and talking to her in her native tongue. What language does Kris speak?
5. At the very end of the movie, what do Doris and Fred see in Susan's dream house that makes them think of Kris?

ANSWERS: 1. Cupid and Blitzen have been switched. Dasher should be to the right of Santa Claus. Donder (as the movie spells it) should have four antler points rather than three. 2. Crack a whip. 3. His beard is real. 4. Dutch. 5. His cane.

WHO SAID IT?

Match the line of dialogue with the character who said it. Some characters

48

may be used more than once; some not at all.

1. "I just turned around and
   there he was."
2. 'I don't think it's lovely."
3. "Maybe I didn't do such a
   wonderful thing after all."
4. "Imagine . . . Macy's Santa Claus
   sending customers to
   Gimbel's."
5. "You're sort of the whole thing
   in miniature."
6. "I always tell the absolute truth."
7. "I speak French, but that doesn't
   make me Joan of Arc."

A. Alfred
B. Kris
C. Fred
D. Mr. Macy
E. Doris
F. Susan
G. Mr. Sawyer

ANSWERS: 1-E, 2-F, 3-C, 4-D, 5-B, 6-B, 8-E.

SUSAN THE CYNIC

1. Which fairy tale does Susan tell Fred she doesn't know?
2. What kind of school does Susan tell Kris she attends.
3. What kind of animal does Kris teach Susan to act like?
4. What does Susan do every night before going to sleep?
5. What does Susan show Kris when he asks her what she wants for
   Christmas?
6. How much of a discount does Susan say her mother gets at Macy's?
7. What does Susan look for in the backyard of her dream house?

ANSWERS: 1. Jack and the Beanstalk. 2. A progressive school. 3. A mon-key. 4. Blows bubble gum. 5. An advertisement for a Cape Cod house on Long Island. 6. Ten percent. 7. A swing on a tree.

IN A WORD

Briefly describe the significance of these words to the plot.

1. Nail biting
2. Football helmet.

3. Fire truck
4. Haslip, Haslip, Mackenzie, Sherman & Haslip
5. Long Island
6. Latent maniacal tendencies
7. Bellevue

ANSWERS: 1. One of Sawyer's nervous habits. 2. What the district attorney's son wants for Christmas. 3. The first toy Kris sends a Macy's customer to another store to buy. 4. Fred's law firm. 5. Where Kris lives and where Susan and Fred would like to live. 6. What Sawyer says Kris has. 7. Where Sawyer takes Kris against his will.

MEET OUR HERO

Answer these questions about Kris Kringle correctly and maybe he'll bring you a nice present.

1. How old does Kris say he is?
2. Who does he list as his next of kin?
3. Where does he say he was born?
4. Kris consistently receives compliments from people about something he owns--what is it?
5. What questions does Kris say are always on the psychological tests?
6. What does Kris always carry?
7. What is Kris' response in court when asked where he lives?
8. When Kris deliberately fails his test at Bellevue, who does he say was the first president?
9. What is Kris' response when Doris asks him if he's had any experience playing Santa Claus?

ANSWERS: 1. "As old as my tongue; a little bit older than my teeth." 2. The eight reindeer. 3. The North Pole. 4. His elegant red Santa Claus suit. 5. How many days in the week? How many fingers do you see? Who was the first president of the United States? 6. A cane. 7. "That's what this hearing will decide." 8. Calvin Coolidge. 9. "Oh, a little!"

WORKING AT MACY'S

1. What is the name of the head of the toy department?

2. By what shortened version of his name do Mr. Macy's executives call him?
3. Though he fancies himself a psychologist, what is Mr. Sawyer actually paid to do?
4. What is the position of Kris' young friend, Alfred?
5. In his so-called therapy with Mr. Sawyer, what does Alfred "discover" is the reason he likes to play Santa Claus?
6. What other Freudian fact about Alfred does Sawyer uncover?
7. What is inside the big books Macys' keeps for its customers?

ANSWERS: 1. Mr. Shellhammer. 2. R.H. 3. Administer intelligence tests. 4. Janitor. 5. A guilt complex. 6. He supposedly hates his father. 7. Advertisements from rival stores.

WHAT HAPPENED NEXT

For this matching quiz, take a plot element from the first column and match it with the plot element from the second column that most closely follows it in the film.

1. Susan watches the parade with Fred.	A. Susan sees Kris speak Dutch to a child.
2. Susan writes a letter to Kris.	B. Kris cleans his beard.
3. Fred takes Susan to see Santa Claus.	C. Doris invites Fred to Thanksgiving dinner.
4. Mr. Macy testifies at Kris' hearing	D. Susan sees her dream house.
5. Kris gives Fred directions for a shortcut home.	E. The post office sends Santa Claus' letters to the courthouse.
6. Susan shows Kris how to blow bubbles.	F. Sawyer is fired.

ANSWERS: 1-C, 2-E, 3-A, 4-F, 5-D, 6-B.

ORDER IN THE COURT

1. What is Kris' response when this District Attorney asks him if he thinks he's Santa Claus?
2. What important witness admits that he believes Kris to be the one and

only Santa Claus?

3. What does Fred do during the trial to upset the ever-practical Doris?
4. Whose son does Fred put on the stand to testify?
5. How many letters does Fred originally produce to prove that the Post Office is delivering Santa Claus' letters to Kris?
6. On what day of the year does the trial end?
7. How many sacks of mail are brought into the courtroom?
8. Where does Judge Harper tell Fred to put all the letters?
9. During the trial, what little surprise makes Kris so happy?
10. What is Charlie, the judge's pal, always chomping on?

ANSWERS: 1. "Of course." 2. Mr. Macy. 3. Quits his job. 4. The District Attorney's. 5. Three. 6. Christmas Eve. 7. Twenty-one. 8. "On my desk." 9. An encouraging letter from Susan and Doris. 10. A big cigar.

HOLIDAY INN

VITAL STATISTICS
Year Released: 1942
Studio: Paramount

Director: Mark Sandrich
Writer: Claude Binyon
Cast: Bing Crosby, Fred Astaire, Marjorie Reynolds, Virginia Dale,
    Walter Abel, and Louise Beavers

Academy Award Nominations: 3
Academy Awards Won: 1

Claim to Fame: Bing Crosby had appeared before in movies with
Irving Berlin songs, and in 1942, he was certainly one of the country's
best-known entertainers. But he had no way of knowing when he
walked onto the set that first morning that *Holiday Inn* would be a life-
changing experience. This little black-and-white musical introduced
the song that was destined to become the biggest-selling record ever,
"White Christmas." It also introduced the words *Holiday Inn* to the
American vocabulary, which a well-known motel chain subsequently
took as its own. The film's two singing-and-dancing couples would be
echoed in a later Crosby-Berlin collaboration, *White Christmas*. A
bevy of holiday songs written especially for the film were premiered in
Holiday Inn, too (though "Easter Parade" already existed).

THE STORY

Crooner Jim Davis (Bing Crosby) wants to quit show business to live on a farm in Connecticut. But his fiancee, Lila Dixon (Virginia Dale), decides to continue in show business with hoofer Ted Hanover (Fred Astaire). Farm life proves harder than Jim anticipated, and he decides to refashion his property as Holiday Inn, a place where people can enjoy the finest in food and entertainment--on holidays only. He's joined by a young singer named Linda Mason (Marjorie Reynolds), who becomes his love interest, as well. Trouble enters when the now-jilted Ted finds himself in need of a new dance partner, and he sets his eyes on Linda--romantically, too. Afraid of losing a second girl to Ted, Jim employs all sorts of trickery and deceit to keep Linda at Holiday Inn. The lure of Hollywood proves strong, however, and Ted and Linda take off for the West Coast. There are a few more plot twists in store before a happy ending comes about and two couples sing and dance on New Year's Eve.

WHAT THE CRITICS SAID

In *Variety*:
"A compact 100 minutes of tiptop filmusical entertainment. . . . Irving Berlin has fashioned some peach [sic] holidays. Mark Sandrich's production and direction are more than half the success of the picture."

In the *New York Times*:
"The man Irving Berlin has been whistling to himself again. . . . He has scribbled no fewer than thirteen tunes. . . . The film has caught the same effortless moods of the music. . . . In Marjorie Reynolds, a very fetching blonde young lady, Mr. Astaire has a new partner who can hold her own at all speeds. . . . It never tries too hard to dazzle; even in the rousing and topical Fourth of July number, it never commits a breach of taste by violently waving the flag."

IRVING BERLIN THE SCREENWRITER?

Well, not exactly. But he was nominated for two Academy Awards in 1942: Best Song ("White Christmas"), which he won, and Original Story, which essentially recognized the underlying concept of a movie and not the script itself. And, indeed, *Holiday Inn* is a great concept. Irving Berlin, the man with his fingers on the pulse of America, thought that a loosely structured movie based on favorite American holidays would be a wonderful framework for new songs. He favored the musical revue--in fact, two other Berlin musicals, *As Thousands Cheer* and *Blue Skies*, also feature similar plot-barely-there formats. With *Holiday Inn*, Berlin had a hit. Its patriotism was a winner in movie theatres coast to coast. So Berlin, who wrote everyone's favorite Easter song ("Easter Parade," from *As Thousands Cheer*), and everyone's favorite patriotic song ("God Bless America"), also came up with the idea for one of the best Christmas films ever.

A CLASSIC SONG

You don't know who to believe. Did Irving Berlin know that "White Christmas" was going to be a legend? Many people connected with the film said that Berlin expected "Be Careful, It's My Heart" to be a hit. And while audiences liked it, it didn't come anywhere near the popularity of such classic Berlin love songs as "What'll I Do?" or "Always." But according to Lawrence Bergreen in his Berlin biography *As Thousands Cheer*, Berlin stood behind "White Christmas" from day one. In the book, Bergreen says that Berlin presented the song to his transcriber, Helmy Kresa. (Berlin couldn't read music and, thus, used a transcriber to set his musical ideas on paper.) "Not only is it the best song I ever wrote," Berlin allegedly said, "It's the best song anybody ever wrote." Berlin may well have been right. American soldiers overseas found the song's simple lyrics symbolic of everything they were fighting for--and wanted to return to. And in Bing Crosby's recordings,

"White Christmas" became the second best-known Christmas song ever, behind "Silent Night."

BEHIND THE SCENES WITH HOLIDAY INN

As we all know, the song "White Christmas" was not an overwhelming hit when it was first released. Two things probably helped it. Irving Berlin got rid of the original opening verse (on the original sheet music), which referred to sitting in Los Angeles and wishing for snow. He wisely realized that this limited the universal appeal of the song. The second factor was beyond Berlin's control. When homesick World War II soldiers heard the tune, its simple, sentimental description of a real American Christmas reminded them of everything they had left behind. It was the soldiers who demanded that the song be played again and again on the radio and who, in fact, made it a hit.

In Lawrence Bergreen's definitive Berlin biography, *As Thousands Cheer*, he relates an amusing anecdote. It seems that Tom Pryor of *Variety* (the newspaper of the film industry) had predicted an early death for Berlin's favorite song, declaring it to be "too schmaltzy." The ever-competitive Berlin never forgot a negative comment, and when he ran into Pryor in 1949--by which time "White Christmas" was well on its way to legendary status--he couldn't resist saying, "Say, Tom. 'White Christmas' is doing pretty good, eh?" We can only assume that Pryor looked appropriately sheepish.

There have been differing stories over the years as to what Bing Crosby's initial reaction was when he glanced at the sheet music to "White Christmas" for the first time. According to one story, he quickly scanned the music, took his pipe out of his mouth, and said, "Irving, this is one you don't have to worry about." But another story says that the devoutly Roman Catholic Crosby wasn't so sure he wanted to sing a Christmas song with such a strong secular bent. Whatever the story, when Crosby went to record the song, he made quick work of it. He was in and out of the studio in an 18-minute recording session.

The story for *Holiday Inn* was Irving Berlin's brainchild, and he was also deeply involved in the development of the picture, choosing the director, stars, etc.

At Irving Berlin's one-hundredth birthday celebration, which was televised but which Berlin did not attend due to bad health, Rosemary Clooney brought down the house when she sang "White Christmas," the little tune Berlin always knew would be a hit.

If you didn't get enough of Crosby singing Berlin tunes in *Holiday Inn* and *White Christmas,* check out the movie *Blue Skies.* In it, Crosby sings 16 Berlin tunes.

Although his recording of "White Christmas" alone would make Crosby a recording legend, he never won a Grammy Award.

In addition to being a beloved entertainer, Crosby was also a shrewd businessman. At his death in 1977, his estimated worth was between $200 and $400 million.

Marjorie Reynolds, who played the role of Linda Mason so delightfully in *Holiday Inn,* had previously starred in films as a brunette under the name Marjorie Moore (her real name was Marjorie Goodspeed). She changed her name to Reynolds in 1937 and became a blonde in the early 1940s, when her career really began to blossom. In *Holiday Inn,* her singing was dubbed by Martha Mears. Reynolds costarred with Crosby one other time, in the 1943 musical *Dixie.* She is perhaps best-known for her television work, particularly as the wife in the 1950s sitcom *Life of Riley.*

In Fred Astaire's autobiography *Steps in Time*, he says of working with

Bing Crosby on *Holiday Inn*: "He surprised me. Having heard that he didn't like to rehearse much, I was amazed when he showed up in practice clothes to rehearse our first song and dance, 'I'll Capture Her Heart.'"

Astaire's own favorite dance number in the movie was "Say It with Firecrackers." Viewing this number, Astaire declared, "I wished the film had been in color."

Astaire commented of his New Year's Eve dance: "Yes, you're right. I took two stiff hookers of bourbon before the first take and one before each succeeding take. I had to fall down on my face and be carried out for the finish. It was hot on that stage, too! All in all, we did it seven times. . . . the last one was the best."

Marjorie Reynolds and Virginia Dale were chosen to costar *because* they were relatively unknown. Astaire and Crosby's salaries were so high that the filmmakers couldn't afford big names in the leading lady roles, too.

After a brief build-up in Hollywood, this was Virginia Dale's last movie--she was normally a nightclub performer.

Paramount publicity said, rather hysterically that *Holiday Inn* contained "the most new music ever presented in a single motion picture."

The beautiful *Holiday Inn* set was designed by Hollywood veteran Hans Dreier. He was nominated for an Oscar twenty times, winning for *Frenchman's Creek, Samson and Delilah*, and *Sunset Boulevard*. *Holiday Inn* was not among his nominations.

TRIVIA QUIZZES

WHO'S WHO

We'll start with a relatively easy one: the names of the characters in the movie. The cast is relatively small, so let's hope you'll score 100 percent on this one!

1.	The singing male lead	A. Gus
2.	The inn's housekeeper	B. Vanderbilt
3.	The ambitious manager	C. Lila
4.	The dancing male lead	D. Ted
5.	The village "cabby"	E. Mamie
6.	The housekeeper's daughter	F. Linda
7.	Jim Hardy's love interest	G. Danny
8.	The housekeeper's son	H. Daphne
9.	Ted Hanover's final partner	I. Jim

ANSWERS: 1-I, 2-E, 3-G, 4-D, 5-A, 6-H, 7-F, 8-B, 9-C.

MEET OUR HERO

As played by Bing Crosby, Jim Hardy is a likable fellow. How well do you know him?

1. How many days a year does Jim want to do nothing?
2. In the opening act, when's he's still part of a trio, what does he carry onstage? (Extra points: what do Ted and Lila carry?)
3. What time does he wake up on the farm?
4. What type of preserves does he unsuccessfully make?
5. What does he smoke?
6. Where is he after a year of working on the farm?
7. What is the name of the turkey he eats for Thanksgiving?
8. When he writes to Linda, how does he sarcastically congratulate her on her engagement to Ted?
9. Where do Ted and Danny try to trap Jim? How does he escape?

ANSWERS: 1. 350. 2. Jim carries candy, Ted carries flowers, and Lila carries a muff. 3. 3:40 a.m. 4. Peach. 5. A pipe. 6. A funny farm (sanitari-

um). *7. Mr. Jones. 8. "I guess that makes your success complete." 9. They lock him in a closet. Jim escapes via the closet's back door.*

BREAKING UP IS HARD TO DO

The plot of Holiday Inn *is one romantic entanglement after another. Any romances that start up are submitted to temptations, trickery, and deceit before the happy ending. Do you remember all the comings and goings?*

1. At the beginning of the movie, who's engaged to whom?
2. How does Jim find out Lila's leaving him?
3. How does Ted find out Lila's leaving him?
4. What two things does Ted proceed to do?
5. On what holiday does Ted fail to find his mystery partner?
6. On what holiday does Ted successfully find his mystery partner?
7. On what holiday does Ted move into the inn?
8. Why does Linda leave Jim?
9. How does Jim find out Linda is engaged to Ted?
10. According to Danny, how long does it take Jim to win Linda back?

ANSWERS: 1. Jim and Lila are engaged. 2. Danny Reed, their manager, spills the beans. 3. A telegram. 4. Gets drunk and shows up at Holiday Inn. 5. Lincoln's Birthday. 6. Valentine's Day. 7. Easter. 8. Because he deceives her about the Hollywood talent scouts being at the inn. 9. He reads about it in a magazine.

THOSE FABULOUS BERLIN SONGS

Irving Berlin wrote wonderfully appropriate songs for each of the holidays featured in Holiday Inn. *Can you match the song to its holiday? Note: some holidays have more than one song.*

1.	"Abraham"	A.	New Year's Day
2.	"Let's Start the New Year Right"	B.	Lincoln's Birthday
3.	"I've Got Plenty to be Thankful For"	C.	Valentine's Day
4.	"Easter Parade"	D.	Washington's Birthday
5.	"Let's Say It with Firecrackers"	E.	Easter
6.	"White Christmas"	F.	Fourth of July
7.	"Happy Holiday"	G.	Thanksgiving

8. "I Can't Tell A Lie"   H.   Christmas
9. "Be Careful, It's My Heart"
10. "Song of Freedom"

ANSWERS: 1-B, 2-A, 3-G, 4-E, 5-F, 6-H, 7-A, 8-D, 9-C, 10-F.

SING ALONG WITH IRVING

Irving Berlin wrote some pretty witty lyrics when he wasn't writing beautiful melodies. In Holiday Inn, *these songs are perfect for the characters who sing them. Let's see how well you listened.*

1. In "Easter Parade," what kind of poem does Jim Hardy say he could write?
2. In the song "I've Got Plenty to Be Thankful For," what gourmet delicacy does Jim Hardy say he's happy without?
3. In the song "You're Easy to Dance With," what can Ted Hanover hardly keep his mind on?
4. At the end of the movie, Ted changes a song line from "Over my dead body" to "Over my _____ body." Fill in the blank.
5. In that same song, what nasty nickname does Ted give Lila?
6. In the montage sequence that shows Jim's feeble efforts at farming, what song do we hear Bing Crosby sing?

ANSWERS: 1. A sonnet. 2. Caviar. 3. "My feet." 4. "Scarred." 5. Miss Hit-and Run. 6. "Lazy."

WHAT HAPPENED NEXT?

Take a plot element from the first column and match it with the plot element from the second column that most closely follows it in the movie.

1. Danny and Ted trap Jim   A.   Jim goes to Hollywood.
2. Jim and Linda get buried under   B.   Ted moves into the inn.
    snow.   C.   Jim sings "White Chrismas"
3. Ted gets drunk.   D.   Linda makes a run for it.
4. Jim and Linda sing "Holiday Inn". E.   Jim finally wins Linda
5. Jim listens to his Thanksgiving
    song.

6.	Danny orders orchids for Lila.	F.	Jim picks at his meal.
7.	Jim and Linda share a table at the Club Pierre.	G.	Jim moves to the farm.
8.	Jim quits show business.	H.	Ted and Linda dance together.
9.	Mamie tells Jim off in the kitchen	I.	Jim and Linda work together.
10.	Jim sings "Easter Parade."	J.	Linda goes to the Club Pierre.

ANSWERS: 1-E, 2-C, 3-H, 4-I, 5-F, 6-J, 7-D, 8-G, 9-A, 10-B.

A FINE ROMANCE

In spite of all their problems, Jim and Linda finally get together at the end of the movie. Trace the rocky path of their courtship.

1. Where do Jim and Linda meet?
2. What does Linda say to Jim to make him think she's a celebrity?
3. What is Jim doing when Linda arrives at the inn?
4. On what holiday do Jim and Linda first work together?
5. What is Jim doing as he proposes to Linda?
6. What is the name of the song that Jim writes for Linda?
7. How does Jim sabotage Linda's Washington's Birthday performance?
8. What misplaced item on the movie set does Jim say only he and Linda would notice?
9. What three things let Linda know Jim is on the set?

ANSWERS: 1. The Club Pierre. 2. "I'm Linda Mason." 3. Working on the roof. 4. New Year's Eve. 5. Putting blackface paint on her. 6. "Be Careful, It's My Heart" 7. By fooling around with the tempo. 8. The Christmas tree. 9. He leaves his pipe on the piano, whistles, and begins to sing.

WHO SAID IT?

Match these lines of dialogue with the characters who said them. Some characters will be used more than once; some not at all.

1.	"He didn't own millions; he *owed* millions."	A.	Mamie
2.	"We were just looking for the back of a girl we don't know."	B.	Jim
		C.	Linda

3. "But the world can't do that to us!"   D.   Ted
4. "You're a fake and I'm a phony."   E.   Lila
5. "Dedicating our lives to making people   F.   Danny
      happy with our feet."
6. "Well, I guess I'm sort of engaged."
7. "Loose . . . looking like they don't care."

ANSWERS: 1-B, 2-D, 3-F, 4-C, 5-E, 6-C, 7-F.

MINOR DISASTERS

You may not have noticed it, but Holiday Inn *is quite a violent movie. Here's some trivia on some of the more explosive incidents.*

1. In the farming sequence, what is Jim carrying when he stumbles down the steps of the inn?
2. What two things does Jim throw against the bedroom wall on the day he decides to quit farming?
3. After he throws those two items, what does he rip?
4. What happens to the peach preserves Jim makes? How many jars are there?
5. What does Jim do when Linda arrives at the inn the first time?
6. What do Jim and Linda find themselves buried in when she arrives at the inn?
7. The first time Ted and Linda dance together, what stage prop do they break?

ANSWERS: 1. Firewood. 2. An alarm clock and a lamp. 3. His pillow. 4. They explode. There are three jars. 5. Falls off the roof. 6. Snow. 7. A large paper heart.

BITS & PIECES

Here are some general questions about Holiday Inn *to keep the true aficionado on his or her toes.*

1. What kind of cooking is promised at Holiday Inn?
2. Where is the flower shop where Linda works located?
3. What are Lila's favorite flowers? How many does Danny order?

4. Who got first billing in the original three-person act of Lila Dixon, Ted Hanover, and Jim Hardy?
5. Of the three exploding preserves, which one exploded first: left, middle, or right?
6. Whose jar of preserves exploded most loudly?
7. Who is Linda supposed to ask for when she arrives at the Club Pierre?
8. Who got first billing in the movie credits for Holiday Inn?
9. In what town did Jim Hardy open Holiday Inn?
10. Who is the guest of honor at the inn in the movie's final scene?

ANSWERS: 1. Home cooking. 2. The airport. 3. Orchids. He orders a dozen. 4. Ted Hanover. 5. The middle one was first. 6. Danny's. 7. Francois. 8. Bing Crosby. 9. Midville, Connecticut. 10. Ted Hanover.

A CHRISTMAS STORY

VITAL STATISTICS
Year Released: 1983
Studio: MGM

Director: Bob Clark
Writers: Jean Shepherd, Leigh Brown, and Bob Clark
Cast: Peter Billingsley, Darren McGavin, and Melinda Dillon

Academy Award Nominations: 0
Academy Awards Won: 0

Claim To Fame: Released with an utter lack of fanfare during the holiday movie deluge of 1983, this warm, witty piece of nostalgia was a hit, due in no small part to Jean Shepherd's unmatched gift for exaggeration. Audiences responded to it so warmly that MGM re-released the film to theaters the following Christmas--definitely not the usual studio practice. The everyday events of a young boy growing up in Indiana in the 1940s become the stuff of myth and legend in Shepherd's dramatic retelling. Darren McGavin (TV's former *Night Stalker*) is memorable as the boy's grouchy father, who cares more than you think he does. Peter Billingsley was first-rate as Ralph Parker, the little boy who repeatedly endures the sound of those hated words, "You'll shoot your eye out!"

THE STORY

Young Ralph Parker (Peter Billingsley) has a mission: to get a Red Ryder air rifle for Christmas. But there are too many obstacles to overcome. His mother (Melinda Dillon) doesn't think they're safe. His father, also known as the Old Man (Darren McGavin) doesn't even seem to notice Ralph wants one--he's too busy fixing malfunctioning appliances and entering contests. His teacher gives him a bad grade on his essay extolling the virtues of the Red Ryder air rifle. And then there's the school bully. It seems Ralph can't walk to and from school without running into this potential homicidal maniac. All seems lost until Ralph decides to let Santa Claus (whom he refers to as "The Big Man" and "The Connection") know of his utmost desires. Will Ralph get what he wants for Christmas? Will the school bully ever get his comeuppance? Will Ralph's little brother ever finish his dinner? Will Ralph's father win the battle of the furnace? Stay tuned.

WHAT THE CRITICS SAID

In the *New York Times*:
"There are a number of small, unexpectedly funny moments in 'A Christmas Story,' but you have to possess the stamina of a pearl diver to find them. . . . Just about everything that is good in 'A Christmas Story' can be attributed to Jean Shepherd, the novelist and radio-television humorist who wrote the book . . . from which the screenplay was adapted. . . . Mr. Clark . . . does not have a light touch."

In the *Chicago Tribune*:
"A delightful motion picture that is doomed to box office failure. It would appear to be a children's film, but it really is a whimsical piece for adults about childhood. . . . 'A Christmas Story' is full of delightful characters and performances. . . . Any message is secondary to the constant delight of nostalgia that flows through every scene. It's like look-

ing through a faded family snapshot album. . . . a movie with a golden glow."

BEHIND THE SCENES WITH A CHRISTMAS STORY

In an interview on the TNT cable network in 1994 (during which the film was referred to as "our generation's Christmas classic"), Darren McGavin confided that every bit of snow in the movie was artificial. According to McGavin, director Bob Clark waited and waited for the snow to fall on the movie's location cities--Toronto, Ontario, and Cleveland, Ohio--but it just wouldn't. The scene in which Ralph wakes up on Christmas morning and opens his bedroom window to a winter wonderland was a major accomplishment on the part of the film's technical crew.

The weather didn't cooperate, but the people of Cleveland certainly did. Many citizens donated antique vehicles to add to the vintage look of the film.

In the playground scene (filmed at Victoria School in St. Catherine's, Ontario), Flick's tongue was "stuck" to the pole with suction. And if you look carefully when Miss Shields is questioning the children about Flick, you can see that a boy sitting behind Ralph is wearing a black rubber digital watch circa 1983. The story, of course, takes place in the 1940s.

In the book and in the movie, Ralph lives in fictional Hohman, Indiana, which Shepherd describes as a mill town. He based it on his real hometown of Hammond, Indiana. Hammond really does have a Warren G. Harding School and a Cleveland Avenue.

Almost every year, Turner Network Television plays the film continuously for an entire day during December. This round-the-clock film has earned the movie a devoted fan base.

If Melinda Dillon and Darren McGavin had been the real-life parents of Ralph and Randy, there would have been a big age gap between them. He was 61 and she was 44 when the film was made. By the way, Jack Nicholson was considered for the role of the Old Man.

The book *In God We Trust, All Others Pay Cash,* which serves as the basis for the movie, is a work of fiction, not Jean Shepherd's autobiography, as many people assume. (The book is generally considered autobiographical, though, and Shepherd even dedicated it to his mother and "kid brother.") In the book, the grown-up Ralph returns to his hometown and spends the evening reminiscing at the local bar with Flick, who is now a bartender.

It's fun comparing the book *In God We Trust* with the movie to see what changes were made in turning the book into a film. Of the book's 264 pages, only about 30 provide material for the movie, most of these from a chapter entitled, "Duel in the Snow, or Red Ryder Nails the Cleveland Street Kid."

In the book, Ralph slips the ad for the air rifle into his mother's copy of *Screen Romance.* In the movie, *Look* was substituted. Perhaps the movie's prop people were unable to find a copy of *Screen Romance* at antique stores!

In the movie, Ralph tells his mother at breakfast that Flick is getting an air rifle for Christmas. In the book, he confides to the reader that this a complete lie.

In the movie, Ralph's dad tries to act pleased upon receiving a can of Simoniz on Christmas morning. In the book, we learn that the Simoniz is from Ralph. It is also Ralph who gives Randy his beloved toy zeppelin.

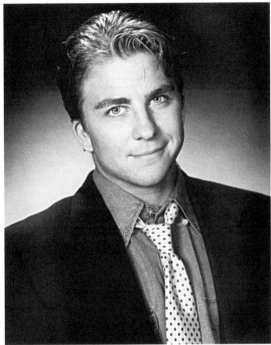

All grown up, Peter Billingsley was 12 years old when he played Ralphie in A Christmas Story. *The producers of the movie game him a Red Ryder rifle when filming was complete.*

(Kingsley)

Ralph's teacher in the movie is Miss Shields. In the book, her name is Miss Bodkin, and she is a less harsh grader than Miss Shields. She gives Ralph a grade of B (rather than Miss Shields' C+) on his Christmas theme.

Everyone remembers the horrible department-store Santa in the movie. In the book, the offensive Santa adds to his sins by smoking Camel cigarettes.

Remember the man who tells Ralph and Randy, "The back of the line starts back there"? The actor who played the man was author Jean Shepherd. Also, when the Old Man goes outside to get a better look at his major award, his neighbor is played by director Bob Clark.

In the book, Ralph doesn't have to wait until Christmas morning to open his gifts, because the family opens their gifts on Christmas Eve. This means, of course, that rather than receiving his gun and getting to play with it right away, Ralph has to wait until the following morning. Clearly, this delay would not have made good cinema, so the screenwriters had all the excitement take place on Christmas morning.

Also mindful of what is funny on-screen, Shepherd changed the gift Ralph receives from the despised, unseen Aunt Clara. We all remember the embarrassing pink bunny suit Ralph is forced to wear in the movie; in the book, he merely has to contend with a pair of bunny slippers.

If the Bumpus hounds look appropriately undisciplined, it's no surprise. According to Darren McGavin, they were not trained movie dogs and reacted with ecstasy when let loose on the Christmas turkey.

In a short article summarizing offbeat holiday films in its December 1993, issue, *Entertainment Weekly* gave *A Christmas Story* a grade of A-. Better than Ralph's Christmas theme!

Midwest humorist Jean Shepherd was born on July 26, 1929. In addition to writing, he also did some acting. He and his wife, Leigh Brown, wrote the script for the movie along with director Clark. Surprisingly, Shepherd did a great deal of writing over the years for *Playboy*. He died in 1999.

Shepherd also had a gift for memorable titles. Some of his other books are *The America of George Ade* (1961), *Wanda Hickey's Night of Golden Memories* (1971), *The Ferrari in the Bedroom* (1973), and *A Fistful of Fig Newtons* (1981).

The gun Ralph requests never actually existed and was created just for the movie. It now resides at the St. Catherine's Museum in Ontario.

The message Ralph decodes is not only disappointing, it's inaccurate. Supposedly, the number twelve stands for the letter *B*. Although the code Ralph writes down contains more than one twelve, the message "Be sure to drink your Ovaltine" contains only one *B*.

Peter Billingsley has commented that playing Ralph was rather difficult since so much of the story is narrated by the adult Ralph. Therefore he had to constantly show with his facial expressions what was going on in Ralphie's mind.

On Christmas morning, there is a jar of pickles on the table even though we don't see Mother bring the jar up from the basement until a few moments later. And in the final scene, the Chinese restaurant owner is standing at the end of the table as he conducts the chorus of waiters. As the scene cuts into the restaurant, he is standing behind the table, even though we haven't missed one note of the song.

The film was released in mid-November 1983 and by Christmas it had been pulled from theaters. By that time, audiences were hearing how wondeful it was, so MGM put it back in limited release until January 1984.

During the scene when Ralph presents Miss Shields with her fruit basket, the arrangement of the fruit changes several times, though neither of them has touched it.

When Mother breaks the Old Man's lamp, we see her holding large chunks of the lamp minus its fishnet stocking. After showing the Old Man's reaction, the scene cuts back to Mother holding a lamp broken in a completely different way--and the stocking is back. Also, although Mother refers to it as a plastic lamp, when it breaks it sound like glass.

When asked as a young adult what the greatest Christmas gift he had ever received was, Peter Billingsley promptly replied, "the Genuine

Red Ryder Model Air Rifle I received from the film's producers!"

Peter Billingsley and costar Ian Petrella (Randy) loved shooting the department store scene because they could go down the slide again and again between takes.

According to Peter Billingsley, the house used as the Parker residence was only used for exterior shots--inside it was gutted. When the characters had to emerge from the house, they were quite chilly, as it was only heated inside with a few space heaters.

TRIVIA QUIZZES

BITS AND PIECES

Here's a little warm-up. How much do you know about A Christmas Story?

1. What studio released the film?
2. Who received first billing?
3. In what state does the movie take place?
4. What is the name of the department store featured in the movie?
5. In the department store Christmas parade, characters from what classic 1939 film are featured?
6. What Disney character is featured in the same parade?
7. What is the main character's name?
8. What is his brother's name?
9. What street do they live on?
10. What is the last name of their next-door neighbors?
11. What smelly pets do the next-door neighbors own?

ANSWERS: 1. MGM. 2. Melinda Dillon. 3. Indiana. 4. Higbee's. 5. The Wizard of Oz. 6. Mickey Mouse. 7. Ralph Parker. 8. Randy. 9. Cleveland Street. 10. Bumpus. 11. A pack of hound dogs.

MEET OUR HERO

The bespeckled Ralph is no wimp, as we learn during the movie. Here are some questions about a boy of rare courage and determination.

1. Here's an easy one: what does Ralph want for Christmas?
2. What toy does he tell his mother he'd settle for?
3. What is his favorite radio show?
4. At what time does that radio show air?
5. What is the disappointing message Ralph decodes?
6. What does Ralph refer to as "the Holy Grail of Christmas Gifts"?
7. What soap does Ralph's mother use on him when he utters "the Queen Mother of Dirty Words"?
8. Into which of his mother's magazines does Ralph slip an advertisement for the Red Ryder air rifle?

ANSWERS: 1. A Red Ryder 200-shot Range Model Air Rifle. 2. Tinker Toys. 3. Little Orphan Annie. 4. 6:45 p.m. 5. "Be sure to drink your Ovaltine." 6. The air rifle, of course. 7. Lifebuoy. 8. Look.

THE OLD MAN

1. What kind of car does the Old Man drive?
2. What household appliance is he always fighting with?
3. According to Ralph, what does the old man buy by the gross?
4. What is the Old Man's favorite pastime?
5. What "major award" does the Old Man win?
6. What is the name of the Lone Ranger's nephew's horse?
7. What does the Old Man receive for Christmas from his wife?
8. Where does he hide Ralph's as-yet-unopened air rifle?
9. How long does it take him to change the tire?
10. What language does the Old Man mistake the word *fragile* for?
11. What is the old man's greatest vice?

ANSWERS: 1. Oldsmobile. 2. The furnace. 3. Fuses. 4. Doing crossword puzzles. 5. A lamp with a base shaped like a woman's fishnet-stocking clad leg. 6. Victor. This is an answer in one of the Old Man's crossword puzzles. 7. A blue bowling bowl. 8. Between his desk and the wall. 9. Eight minutes. 10. Italian. 11. He swears.

SCHOOL DAYS

1. What school does Ralph attend?
2. What is his teacher's name?
3. What are the names of his two best friends?
4. What is the name of the school bully?
5. What is the bully's distinguishing physical characteristic?
6. What is the topic of the theme Ralph's teacher assigns?
7. What grade does Ralph dream of receiving?
8. What grade does he actually receive?
9. What does Ralph give his teacher as a kind of bribe?
10. What does Ralph's teacher write at the bottom of his theme paper?
11. What is the color of the binder Ralph places his theme in?
12. What is the name of the school bully's "crummy little toady"?
13. What is his distinguishing physical characteristic?
14. According to Ralph, what is the most serious dare?

ANSWERS: 1. Warren G. Harding Elementary School. 2. Miss Shields. 3. Flick and Schwartz. 4. Scut (not Scott) Farkus. 5. He has yellow eyes, according to Ralph. 6. "What I Want for Christmas." 7. A+. 8. C+. 9. A very large fruit basket. 10. "You'll shoot your eye out." 11. Red. 12. Grover Dill. 13. Green teeth (again, according to Ralph). 14. A triple dog dare.

NATIONAL LAMPOON'S CHRISTMAS VACATION

VITAL STATISTICS
Year Released: 1989
Studio: Warner Brothers

Director: Jeremiah S. Chechik
Writer: John Hughes
Cast: Chevy Chase, Beverly D'Angelo, Randy Quaid, Juliette Lewis, Doris Roberts, E. G. Marshall, Diane Ladd, Julia Louis-Dreyfus, and Brian Doyle Murphy

Academy Award Nominations: 0
Academy Awards Won: 0

Claim to Fame: The first Christmas movie to be based on a previously existing film series. With the name *National Lampoon* attached to the title, this was a movie that was clearly going to be full of sight gags, pratfalls, and sometimes crude humor. But the filmmakers also knew that audiences expect a certain amount of sentiment at Christmas, and that combination of wildness and warmth made this movie a huge hit. In its initial release it made $71 million, and it has continued to find a new audience on television, videocassette, and DVD. It is one of the most popular Christmas comedies.

THE STORY

Pity poor Clark Griswold. All he wants to do is give his family a fun, old-fashioned Christmas, but it seems he just can't. His kids have gotten to the age where they think Christmas is corny. His parents and in-laws are staying with him, and--naturally--the two couples don't get along. Then his no-good, out-of-work cousin-in-law, Eddie, shows up with his mangy family in their decrepit RV. Even the elaborate Christmas lights Clark has stapled to the house don't work at first. And last, but certainly not least in Clark's eyes, is the fact that he still hasn't received the Christmas bonus he's counting on to cover the huge down payment he's made on a built-in swimming pool. Just when he thinks it can't get any worse, his loyal family comes through for him and shows him that they do appreciate his efforts to make the "Griswold Family Christmas" an event to treasure.

WHAT THE CRITICS SAID

In the *Chicago Sun-Times*:
" . . . the parts don't fit. Maybe the movie's problem is with the director, Jeremiah S. Chechik, a first-timer at feature length. . . . You have the odd sensation, watching this movie, that it's straining to get off the ground but simply doesn't have the juice."

In the *Washington Post*:
"Chase presides over this uneven but amiable slapstick comedy, a decked-out domestic caper that both celebrates and debunks ye olde yuletide chestnuts. . . . *Christmas Vacation* may not be a fancy package, but it is a diverting stocking stuffer."

In the *New York Times*:
"The direction . . . displays comic timing that is uncertain at best. In spite of all this, however, the Griswolds do occasionally have their moments."

BEHIND THE SCENES WITH
NATIONAL LAMPOON'S CHRISTMAS VACATION

Though the film is clearly supposed to take place in a suburb of Chicago, the Griswolds drive through mountainous scenery to get their tree. No surprise there--most of the film was actually shot in and around Breckenridge, Colorado.

The "Christmas tree farm" is really the grounds of the Breckenridge Golf Course, designed by Jack Nicklaus.

It's a Wonderful Life is featured within the movie in two subtle ways. Like George Bailey, Clark has a loose newel post on his staircase (which he decisively saws off). And this film also had a Capra on crew: assistant director Frank Capra III is Frank Capra's grandson.

The home of the obnoxious yuppies Margo and Todd was also home to the Murtaugh family in the *Lethal Weapon* movies.

In the previous two *Vacation* movies, Rusty was the Griswolds' oldest child and Audrey was the youngest. In this one, of course, they're reversed. And as many people have noted, different actors play the Griswold children in every movie.

Johnny Galecki, who played young Rusty, is best known as Darlene's boyfriend, David, on the TV show *Roseanne.*

Before she was an actress, Beverly D'Angelo was a jazz singer (she sings quite well in the opening scene) and an animator for Hanna-Barbera.

As the star of two previous *Vacation* movies, Chevy Chase was very involved in the pre-production of this film, sharing his own Christmas memories with John Hughes and helping to select the cast.

Chase said at the time the film was released: "This is what Christmas is like at my house. Too many people. Too many presents. Too much food."

The crew of this film had the usual problems in making things look appropriately snowy. For the first few weeks of filming, there was hardly any snow in Breckenridge, so the crew literally had to move the snow around. Then a blizzard hit, dumping more than six feet of snow in six days.

Though you can't see much of it, the Griswolds' Christmas Eve feast was prepared by Wendy Blasdel, a former chef at Spago's. Let's hope she really knows how to cook a turkey.

Like Chevy Chase, Randy Quaid is a *Saturday Night Live* alumnus, appearing on that show from 1985 to 1986.

Just asking: why do Audrey and Rusty have to share the double bed in Audrey's room (much to Audrey's disgust) when they could have used the bunk beds in Rusty's room and let Grandpa Arthur and Grandma Frances share the double bed?

The street the Griswolds live on has been used in many Warner Brothers productions, including the old *Blondie* movies. Seems appropriate, given that Clark is a bit of a Dagwood himself.

Todd, Clark's obnoxious next-door neighboor, was played by Nicholas Guest, the brother of Second City veteran Christopher Guest. That makes him Jamie Lee Curtis' brother-in-law.

Randy Quaid and Beverly D'Angelo had previously costarred in a 1984 telecast of Tennessee Williams' *Streetcar Named Desire*. D'Angelo played Blanche DuBois and Quaid played Stanley Kowalski.

When the film was released, *New York Times* critic Janet Maslin said it was "tacky." That may not have been East Coast snobbery talking. When it comes to technical flaws, the film seems to have more than its share.

For example, when Clark starts down the hill on his saucer sled after greasing it up, you can easily see the thick wire pulling the sled. Later, when Uncle Lewis drops the match by the sewer, you can see the rope that launches him into the air.

In an aerial exterior shot of the Griswold house, Eddie's RV is parked in the driveway. Unfortunately, Eddie and clan don't arrive until later in the film.

When the Santa Claus front lawn decoration is launched in the air in the final scene, you can actually see a faint box around the sleigh where the special effects people "dragged" the sleigh across the moon.

In several scenes, the rough ceiling rafters of the dining room set are clearly visible. Since the dining room doesn't have a "country" look, this is obviously a mistake.

Clark is eating dinner while Uncle Lewis is in the living room lighting his cigar. But, though the tree is visible from the dining room, Uncle Lewis is nowhere to be seen. In the next shot from the dining room, the tree has disappeared altogether, though the fire Uncle Lewis causes is easily seen.

When Clark loses his temper about his Christmas bonus, a crew member's head passes by the bottom left corner of the screen.

And finally, when Clark cuts the ropes on the Christmas tree in the living room, you can see large wooden poles connected to the branches of the tree as they burst through the windows.

But, after all, let's give director Jeremiah S. Chechik a break. This was his first film, and before this, he was a fashion photographer.

TRIVIA QUIZZES

MEET OUR HERO

Everyone knows that Clark is a well-intentioned bumbler. What else do you know about the head of the Griswold clan?

1. What is his full name?
2. What professional sports team's logo adorns the baseball cap Clark wears throughout the movie?
3. What did he forget to bring to the Christmas tree farm?
4. What magazine is he reading in bed near the beginning of the film?
5. What product has he just developed at work that Mr. Shirley clearly thinks is a winner?
6. What Looney Tunes character is featured on Clark's coffee cup at work?
7. What is Ellen's nickname for Clark?
8. When Clark goes sledding with his family, he winds up in the parking lot of what store?
9. Instead of a cash bonus, what does Clark get from the company?
10. When Mr. Shirley finally changes his mind about the bonus, how much does he add to Clark's previous bonus?
11. What does Clark use to put out the fire on Uncle Lewis' back?
12. How many years has Clark been with his company?

ANSWERS: 1. Clark Wilhelm Griswold, Jr. 2. Chicago Bears. 3. A saw. 4. People. 5. "A non-nutritive cereal varnish." 6. Tasmanian Devil. 7. Sparky. 8. Wal-Mart. 9. A membership in the Jelly-of-the-Month Club. 10. Twenty percent. 11. The living room curtains. 12. Seventeen years.

MEET THE FAMILY

Though Clark is trying to give his family the perfect Christmas, they're the cause of many of his problems. Here's some questions about his extended clan.

1. Audrey has a poster of what rock group in her bedroom?
2. During the movie, Rusty wears clothing featuring two Midwestern teams. Name them.
3. What Christmas movie does Rusty watch on TV?
4. What two unusual items does Aunt Bethany wrap as presents?
5. What are the names of Eddie and Catherine's two children?
6. What are the names of the four grandparents?
7. According to Ellen, what do the two grandmothers always say about each other?
8. Which grandparent has hemmorhoids?
9. Which grandmother often has a drink in her hand?
10. What is the year of the black-and-white home movie Clark watches in the attic?
11. Who finally figures out how to light the outside Christmas lights? What needs to be done?
12. How many years has cousin Eddie been out of work?

ANSWERS: 1. Guns 'N' Roses. 2. University of Illinois Illini and Chicago Blackhawks. 3. It's a Wonderful Life. 4. Her cat and a Jell-O mold. 5. Rocky and Ruby Sue. 6. Arthur and Francis (Ellen's parents) and Nora and Clark, Sr. (Clark's parents) 7. Francis says that Nora buys cheap hot dogs; Nora says that Francis waxes her upper lip. 8. Francis. 9. Francis. 10. 1955. 11. Ellen; she flips the switch on in the garage. 12. Seven.

CELEBRATING THE SEASON

Clark does manage to provide some Christmas cheer. Here's a rundown of some of the ways the Griswolds celebrate Yuletide.

1. How many total lightbulbs does Clark put on the house?
2. What three decorations are on the front lawn?
3. How many trees does Clark wind up bringing into the house by the end of the movie?
4. What child's toy is used throughout the movie to show the changing dates?
5. What decoration are the two grandmothers seen working on soon after they arrive?
6. What classic Bing Crosby Christmas song is featured in the movie?
7. What drink does Clark share with Eddie?
8. What is unusual about the drinking glasses they use?

9. Where does Clark shop for Ellen's Christmas gifts?
10. What is wrong with the turkey Catherine cooks for Christmas Eve dinner?
11. Instead of grace, what does Aunt Bethany lead the family in at the dinner table?
12. Later, what song does she sing outside?

ANSWERS: 1. 25,000.   2. A santa, eight tiny reindeer, and a sign that says "Merry Christmas."   3. Two.   4. A dollhouse.   5. A gingerbread house. 6. "Mele Kalikimaka."   7. Eggnog.   8. They're Marty Moose glasses from Wally World, the theme park in the first Vacation film.   9. Marshall Field's. 10. It's completely overcooked.   11. The Pledge of Allegiance.   12. "The Star-Spangled Banner."

WHO SAID IT?

Match the line of dialogue with the person who said it.

1. "Put it over there with the others, Greaseball."	A. Rusty
2. "We're at the threshold of hell!"	B. Ellen
3. "I have to eat so I can take my back pill."	C. Margo
4. "That thing wouldn't fit in our backyard."	D. Grandpa Art
5. "Do you know how sick and twisted that is?	E. Audrey
6. "You about ready to do some kissin'?"	F. Mr. Shirley
7. "We have plenty of room."	G. Eddie
8. "I hope he falls and breaks his neck."	H. Clark

ANSWERS: 1-F, 2-H, 3-D, 4-A, 5-E, 6-G, 7-B, 8-C.

HOME ALONE

VITAL STATISTICS
Year Released: 1990
Studio: Twentieth-Century Fox

Director: Chris Columbus
Writer: John Hughes
Cast: Macaulay Culkin, Joe Pesci, Daniel Stern, Catherine O'Hara,
    John Heard, and Roberts Blossom

Academy Award Nominations: 2
Academy Awards Won: 0

Claim to Fame: This little film came out of nowhere to be the most successful comedy of all-time, up to that point. It made a superstar out of Macaulay Culkin (he subsequently became the highest-paid child actor of all time), and his notoriety only increased when word spread of the hard-nosed tactics of his father, who also acted as his agent. The film, in spite of its overwhelming popularity, also drew a lot of criticism for its excessive violence--especially in the midst of a film that advertised itself as a family Christmas movie.

THE STORY

Poor little Kevin McCallister (Macaulay Culkin). Not only does he have to go to Paris for Christmas, but his nasty Uncle Frank is in town, his family isn't speaking to him, and he's scared of Mr. Marley (Roberts Blossom), the old man who lives next door. So when Kevin's entire family inadvertently leaves for vacation without him, it's little wonder he thinks that his wish to make them disappear has actually come true. He has a great time at first, all alone in his luxurious suburban home, until he gets wind of the plans of two incompetent burglars called Harry (Joe Pesci) and Marv (Daniel Stern), who plan to break into Kevin's home on Christmas Eve. Kevin decides it's time to grow up and defend his house--which he does with brilliant success. He also helps Mr. Marley, reunite with *his* family, and learns to appreciate his own family, too.

BEHIND THE SCENES WITH HOME ALONE

Writer John Hughes began his career as a writer on the acerbic comic magazine *National Lampoon*.

Hughes and director Chris Columbus have set other films during Christmas, among them *Gremlins, National Lampoon's Christmas Vacation,* and *Planes, Trains, and Automobiles.*

The film was nominated for two Academy Awards, both nominations going to legendary movie composer John Williams of *Star Wars* and *Jaws* fame. Neither his score nor the lovely song "Somewhere in My Memory" won, however.

The lyrics to "Somewhere in My Memory" were provided by Leslie Bricusse, who had written both the songs and the lyrics for *Scrooge,* the musical version of *A Christmas Carol* starring Albert Finney.

Hughes got the inspiration for *Home Alone* from one of his own films. In *Uncle Buck*, Macaulay Culkin's character is left home alone with his younger sister for a short while before a babysitter he has never met arrives. Culkin is reluctant to let the babysitter into the house and interrogates her through the mail slot on the front door, even demanding to see her driver's license. Hughes took this little idea and turned it into three *Home Alone* movies.

In its original release, *Home Alone* brought in $70 million, nearly saving an ailing 20th-Century Fox Studios.

Though the *Home Alone* movies are supposed to take place in Winnetka, Illinois (based on the luggage tag on Peter's bag in *Home Alone 2*), they were actually filmed in several suburbs of Chicago, including Winnetka, Oak Park, Kenilworth, Wilmette, and Evanston.

The McCallister house actually *is* in Winnetka, Illinois. The family who owns the house had been approached before by Hughes, who wanted to use the house for *Uncle Buck*. The makers of *Opportunity Knocks* also approached the homeowners, asking permission to use their house. The owners finally agreed to the *Home Alone* shoot because they liked Christmas movies.

The real house, however, had rather low ceilings, and a slightly modified version of the interior was built at nearby New Trier West High School in Northfield (it boasted a $50,000 kitchen), as were the McAllister's basement and the interior of the 747 airplane Kate is in when she discovers they've left Kevin behind.

The church that appears to be in Kevin's neighborhood is actually Grace Episcopal Church in Oak Park, Illinois, about 15 miles from where the story is supposed to take place. That's a long way for Kevin to run!

Macaulay Culkin was 10 years old when the movie was made, though Kevin is said to be 8.

The relatively unknown Culkin was paid $100,000 for his work on *Home Alone*. His father negotiated a salary of $4 million when his son signed on for *Home Alone 2*.

At the beginning of *Home Alone*, Kevin says more than once that he's tired of all his brothers and sisters, declaring that when he grows up, "I'm living alone." In real life, he may have felt the same way: he is one of seven siblings.

Catherine O'Hara, who played Kevin's mom, Kate, and Joe Pesci, who played Harry, the man attempting to rob her house, had previously costarred in the Alan Alda film *Betsy's Wedding*.

Joe Pesci said that the relationship between Harry and Marv reminded him of the one between Ralph Kramden and Ed Norton in *The Honeymooners*.

The *Home Alone* shoot began on February 14, 1990, and lasted 13 weeks.

Macaulay Culkin is the nephew of actress Bonnie Bedelia of *Die Hard* fame.

Often, film crews have to add snow where none exists. This was one film shoot where the crew had to remove snow. In the initial days of filming, the snow on the ground was spotty and half-melted, so that's the look director Chris Columbus decided to stick with--until more snow fell. Then the crew had to start removing snow, eventually carting away 375 tons. Later, when they had to add a little more snow, they used potato flakes and airport runway foam.

Everyone remembers the scene in which the McCallister family madly dashes through Chicago's O'Hare Airport trying to catch their airplane.

That scene was actually filmed at O'Hare's Terminal Three. As it turns out, the scenes that supposedly take place at Paris' Orly Airport were also filmed at O'Hare. The airport scenes were shot over four 16-hour days.

To make the airport look appropriately Parisian, the prop crew installed European phones in the terminal. Although the phones didn't work, when shooting wrapped, the crew gathered a sizable amount of loose change dropped in by unsuspecting travelers.

In the film, polka-playing John Candy has missed his flight and, along with his band, rents a U-Haul truck. In real life, actor Candy's flight out of Toronto was cancelled due to snow, and his one-day shoot had to be postponed for several weeks.

Macaulay Culkin (draped in fabric far right.) hides from Harry (Kingsley)
and Marv. This church is actually 15 miles from the house used
as the McCallister home.

In the film, the McCallisters are taking a flight to Paris. On the day the departure scene was shot, the waiting plane was actually about to take off for Hawaii. In addition to the regular weekday travelers at O'Hare, more than 200 extras were used as the McCallister clan ran through the terminal.

In one of the movie's final scenes, Kevin takes refuge in the flooded basement of a neighbor's house that has become the victim of Harry and Marv, the "Wet Bandits." This scene was shot at a local high school's indoor pool.

To enhance the feeling of Kevin being home alone in a large, empty house, the cinematographer used a wide-angle lens for interior shots.

Needless to say, Joe Pesci and Daniel Stern weren't really the recipients of Kevin McCallister's physical torture. The ornaments Marv steps on were made of special breakaway glass, the paint cans Kevin swings at them from the upstairs landing were made of rubber, and the tar on the basement steps was a boiled concoction of licorice and corn syrup.

Remember the scene where the grocery store clerk is peppering Kevin with questions as to why he's shopping alone? In the original theatrical trailer, it is the store manager who grills Kevin--and much less nicely. The lines were delivered by the cashier in a much more tender, humorous way in the final version.

TRIVIA QUIZZES

MEET OUR HERO

Let's see how well you know little Kevin McCallister.

1. How old is Kevin?
2. What is his favorite kind of pizza?

3. What is he afraid of in the basement?
4. What is the name of the movie he watches in the family room? What does he eat while watching it?
5. Where does he get the cash to get him through the days when his family is gone?
6. What does Kevin want to know about the toothbrush he's considering buying?
7. What is he eating for dinner when Harry and Marv arrive the final time? What time do they arrive?
8. What does he leave out for Santa Claus?

ANSWERS: 1. Eight. 2. Plain cheese. 3. The furnace. 4. Angels with Filthy Souls; an enormous ice cream sundae. 5. From a box in Buzz's bedroom. 6. Whether it's approved by the American Dental Association. 7. Microwave macaroni and cheese; 9:00 p.m. 8. Cookies, milk, and carrots.

THE McCALLISTER FAMILY

1. How many siblings does Kevin have? Name them.
2. What are his parents' names? What are the names of his two uncles (one is never seen)?
3. How many people are staying at the McCallister house in the opening scene?
4. From what state did his uncle's family drive in?
5. What is the name of his cousin who supposedly wets the bed?
6. What airline does the extended McCallister family take to Paris?
7. On the plane, what does Kevin's dad admit he forgot to do?
8. What Christmas movie (overdubbed in French) is the McCallister family watching while sitting around the apartment in Paris?
9. What does Frank tell his wife to put in her purse when they're on the airplane?
10. What does Frank tell Kate he left behind?

ANSWERS: 1. Four. Buzz, Megan, Linnie, and Jeff. 2. Kate and Peter; Frank and Rob. 3. Fifteen. 4. Ohio. 5. Fuller, played by Macaulay Culkin's real-life brother, Kieran. 6. American Airlines. 7. Close the garage door. 8. It's a Wonderful Life. 9. Wineglasses and silverware. 10. His reading glasses.

HOME ALONE

AROUND THE NEIGHBORHOOD

1. What is Kevin's address?
2. What is the name of his mysterious neighbor?
3. What is the name of the McCallisters' favorite pizza delivery service? How much do they owe the pizza boy the first time he comes?
4. What does Harry pretend to be in the opening scene?
5. What words are written on the van that Harry and Marv drive?
6. What are the names of the two characters in the scene from *Angels with Filthy Souls* that Kevin watches again and again?
7. By what nickname does Marv want he and Harry to be known?
8. When Kevin runs away from the church to defend his home on the last night, what Christmas carol is played?
9. What does Kevin spill on the basement steps? What does he create on the outdoor steps?
10. After a few attempts, how do Harry and Marv each finally get into the McCallister home?

ANSWERS: 1. 671 Lincoln Boulevard. 2. Mr. Marley. 3. Little Nero's; $122.50. 4. A police officer. 5. Oh-Kay Plumbing & Heating. 6. Johnny and Snakes. 7. "The Wet Bandits." 8. "Carol of the Bells." 9. Tar; ice. 10. Harry comes in through the kitchen door; Marv enters through a window.

WHO SAID IT?

Match the line of dialogue with the character who said it.

1. "I hope we didn't forget anything."   A. Kevin
2. "Very big in Sheboygan."   B. Linnie
3. "You're never too old to be afraid."   C. Uncle Frank
4. "Is it true that French babes don't   D. Kate
   shave their pits?"
5. "This is my house. I have to defend it."   E. Gus
6. "Look what you did, you little jerk!"   F. Jeff
7. "You're what the French call *les*   G. Mr. Marley
   incompetents.*"
8. "Kevin, you're such a disease."   H. Buzz

ANSWERS: 1-D, 2-E, 3-G, 4-H, 5-A, 6-C, 7-B, 8-F.

HOME ALONE 2

VITAL STATISTICS

Year Released: 1992
Studio: Twentieth-Century Fox

Director: Chris Columbus
Writer: John Hughes
Cast: Macaulay Culkin, Joe Pesci, Daniel Stern, Tim Curry,
Rob Schneider, Brenda Fricker, Catherine O'Hara, and
John Heard

Academy Award Nominations: 0
Academy Awards Won: 0

Claim to Fame: The first time a sequel was made to a hit Christmas movie. This one did well at the box office but drew the ire of critics. First, a backlash set in against poor little Macaulay Culkin when word of his astronomical salary got around. Then critics noticed that not only were the plots of the *Home Alone* movies virtually identical, but that some of Kevin's dialogue is duplicated almost exactly from the first film. Parents and critics weren't too fond of the sequel's significantly increased violence, either. Needless to say, kids loved it, and one feels that's what producer John Hughes was counting on. Unfortunately, another sequel was made, and it's hardly worth mentioning. It didn't have the fun, the charm, or Macaulay Culkin.

THE STORY

This year Kevin McCallister (Macaulay Culkin) is prepared. When his family departs for a vacation in Florida, he's in the airport van first. Unfortunately, Kevin gets separated from his family at O'Hare Airport and gets on the wrong plane . . . a plane bound for New York. When Kevin arrives in the Big Apple, he's upset--until he realizes how much fun a vacation on his own will be. He checks into the luxurious Plaza Hotel, makes friends with a homeless pigeon lady (Brenda Fricker), and hires a limo to take him around town, ending up at Duncan's Toy Chest, the city's best toy store. There, he meets the owner (Eddie Bracken), who tells him that all the money the store takes in on Christmas Eve will go to a children's hospital. Therefore, when Kevin runs into his old enemies, Harry (Joe Pesci) and Marv (Daniel Stern)--recently escaped from prison--and learns they plan to rob Duncan's Toy Chest, he once again goes into action, leading them on a merry chase through a houseful of painful and ingenious traps (in this case, his absent uncle's brownstone). Naturally, all ends happily, and Kevin is reunited with the entire family (even Uncle Frank) for a splendid Christmas morning at the Plaza's penthouse suite.

BEHIND THE SCENES WITH HOME ALONE 2

Shooting began in December 1991 and completed in May 1992.

Among the actual Manhattan locations used for the film: Wollman Skating Rink in Central Park, Radio City Music Hall, and the Christmas tree at Rockefeller Center.

Brenda Fricker, the pigeon lady, was given a costume with a cape so that she, too, would look like a bird.

The children's hospital, from which a little boy waves to Kevin, is actually a college building in New York.

The scene where Marv and Harry take Kevin to Central Park was shot at an indoor tennis court in the Chicago area. More than 500 pigeons were needed to attack Harry and Marv, but since pigeons don't fly at night, the scene was shot during the day. Even inside, the pigeons knew the difference.

Real-life employees from the Plaza Hotel appeared in the hotel scenes as extras.

Uncle Rob's street and brownstone were sets built in Los Angeles.

TRIVIA QUIZZES

ANOTHER CHRISTMAS IN THE TRENCHES

1. Where is the McCallister family headed to in *Home Alone 2*?
2. What is the name of the school attended by Kevin and Buzz?
3. What recording device does Kevin make clever use of throughout the movie?
4. What is Kevin so anxious to get out of his father's bag in the airport scene?
5. When Kevin arrives in New York, he takes Polaroid pictures from atop what famous building?
6. How do Marv and Harry arrive in New York?
7. What hotel is advertised as "New York's most exciting hotel experience"?
8. What real-life millionaire appeared in a brief cameo while giving Kevin directions to the hotel lobby?
9. By what name does Marv to be known in this movie?
10. What is the name of the awful hotel where the McCallisters stay in Florida? Why was it chosen?
11. What is Kevin's room number at the Plaza?
12. What nickname does Kevin give to his plan to trap Harry and Marv?
13. Where does Kate find Kevin at the end of the movie?

14. What is the significance of the amount $967.43?

ANSWERS: 1. Florida. 2. St. Gerard's. 3. TalkBoy. 4. Batteries. 5. One of the World Trade Tower buildings. 6. In the back of a fish truck. 7. The Plaza. 8. Donald Trump. 9. "The Sticky Bandits." 10. Villa de Dolphine. It's where Uncle Frank and Aunt Leslie stayed on their honeymoon. 11. 411. 12. Operation Ho-Ho-Ho. 13. The Christmas tree at Rockefeller Center. 14. It's the amount of Kevin's astronomical room service bill.

WHO SAID IT?

Match the line of dialogue with the character who said it.

1. "What is it with you and Christmas trees?"
2. "What a troubled young man."
3. "Wouldn't want to spoil your fun, Mr. Cheapskate."
4. "Hiya, pal!"
5. "I haven't got many friends."
6. "Herbert Hoover once stayed on this floor."
7. "There's an insane guest with a gun!"
8. "You guys give the worst gol' darn wake-up calls."

A. The concierge
B. The pigeon lady
C. Kate
D. Uncle Frank
E. Buzz
F. Kevin
G. Cedric
H. Harry

ANSWERS: 1-C, 2-E, 3-F, 4-H, 5-B, 6-G, 7-A, 8-D.

A CHRISTMAS CAROL

VITAL STATISTICS

Year Released: 1951
Studio: Renown/United Artists

Director: Brian Desmond-Hurst
Writer: Noel Langley
Cast: Alastair Sim, Mervyn Johns, Kathleen Harrison, and Hermione
      Baddeley

Academy Award Nominations: 0
Academy Awards Won: 0

Claim to Fame: The most critically acclaimed of all filmed versions of
A Christmas Carol. As Ebenezer Scrooge, Alastair Sim is positively
scary, with his bulging eyes and sinister smile. The film takes a more
psychological approach to Scrooge's dilemma, dwelling at length on
his past and all the events that turned him into the selfish miser he is.
Unlike some versions, Bob Cratchit is not the focus of much attention.
The final scene, when Scrooge is redeemed, takes some liberties with
Dickens' tale, showing Scrooge romping merrily about his house. This
is a version where Scrooge himself dominates from start to finish.

THE STORY

It is Christmas Eve, and--as he does every year--wealthy, mean-spirited Ebenezer Scrooge (Alastair Sim) is ignoring the holiday. Famous throughout London for his miserly ways and cold heart, Scrooge thinks of Christmas as just another miserable day on the calendar. But this Christmas Eve proves different. When he arrives home, strange voices and visions disturb him, and he is visited by the spirit of his dead business partner, Jacob Marley. Marley tells Scrooge that he has one chance left to redeem himself and change his embittered ways, or his fate will be the same as Marley's: to roam the earth, finally aware of the pain and suffering around him, but powerless to help. Scrooge is then visited by three spirits, of whom the Ghost of Christmas Past has the most profound effect, reminding Scrooge of happy times in his life he had long forgotten. By morning, Scrooge is a changed man, and he vows to keep Christmas in his heart forever.

WHAT THE CRITICS SAID

In the *New York Times*:
"A positive endorsement of Christmas and the sentiment of good will toward men. . . . It should prove a most popular entertainment throughout the approaching holidays. Old Scrooge, played by Britain's distinguished and vastly beloved Alastair Sim, is precisely the dour and crabbed creature that he is in the memorable tale. This [movie] is spooky and sombre, for the most part, except toward the end."

BEHIND THE SCENES WITH A CHRISTMAS CAROL

According to *Antiques & Collectibles Magazine*, a poster of the 1951 Christmas Carol in mint condition sells for more than $150.

In England, Alastair Sim was known for a popular series of movies he made in which he starred as Inspector Hornleigh.

Both Sim and director Brian Desmond-Hurst were 50 years old when they made *A Christmas Carol.*

Kathleen Harrison, who played Scrooge's housekeeper, Mrs. Dilber, often played Cockney servants, though she wasn't even born in London. She also starred in two other Dickens-based films, 1948's *Oliver Twist* and 1952's *The Pickwick Papers.*

South African screenwriter Noel Langley, who mostly worked in British films, was also one of the cowriters of *The Wizard of Oz.* In 1952, he scripted another film based on the work of Charles Dickens, *The Pickwick Papers.*

The movie is also known by the simple title *Scrooge.* (The closing credits read, "The End. Scrooge.") Today it is invariably called *A Christmas Carol*, perhaps to distinguish it from the 1970 musical called *Scrooge* starring Albert Finney.

This version of *A Christmas Carol* has been both criticized and praised for its psychological slant on Scrooge's character. Critics have particularly noted that, in Noel Langley's script, Scrooge's father hates him because his mother died while giving birth to him. (An impossibility, according to Dickens. After all, Scrooge's sister was younger than him.) This explanation of Scrooge's behavior prompted the *New York Times* reviewer to say that the film was "heavy on the Freudian sauce."

The character of Mrs. Dilber, only a minor character in the book (and a decidedly nasty one at that, totally obsessed with selling Scrooge's bed curtains), was turned into a major character in this film version. After Scrooge's transformation to good guy, most of his cheer is shared with Mrs. Dilber, rather than with his downtrodden clerk, Bob Cratchit, as in most versions. Apparently, in keeping with the film's Freudian overtones, Scrooge has finally come to terms with the women in his life.

Michael Hordern, who played Jacob Marlely, was a major star in England and was even knighted--he was Sir Michael Horden. Over the years, he appeared in several well-known films, among them *The VIPs* with Elizabeth Taylor and Richard Burton, *A Funny Thing Happened on the Way to the Forum*, and the TV mini-series *Shogun*, in which he played Friar Domingo.

In the scenes depicting Scrooge's youth, the actor is not Alastair Sim, though he looks an awful lot like him. Young Scrooge was played by George Cole, an actor 25 years Sim's junior. Incidentally, in the musical *Scrooge*, Albert Finney played the young and old Scrooge--but then, he was only 34 when he made his version, as opposed to Sim's 50.

Filmmakers have had fun naming and renaming Scrooge's one-time fiancee, though her name surely seems a moot point. In the old 1931 version starring Sir Seymour Hicks, her name is Belle, just as in the book. By the time of the 1951 Sim version, her name is Alice. (Perhaps after 1939's *Gone with the Wind*, Belle was considered a name strictly for prostitutes.) In the 1971 Albert Finney version, a little authenticity is restored, though the scriptwriter opted for the more elegant Isabel.

Hermione Baddeley, who played the warm and loving Mrs. Cratchit in this version of *A Christmas Carol*, was a veteran British player who starred in innumerable films, many based on Dickens novels. (Sound familiar?) Her career had a more prosaic turn, however, when from 1974 to 1977 she was a regular in the TV sitcom *Maude*, playing Maude's maid Nell Naugatuck.

TRIVIA QUIZZES

MEET OUR HERO

Don't get cocky! You don't really know Scrooge until you've studied Alastair Sim's portrayal of him.

1. What carol does Scrooge stop a group of young boys from singing?
2. When is quitting time at Scrooge & Marley's?
3. Other than accounting tasks, what is Bob Cratchit expected to help his boss with?
4. Why does Scrooge decide not to have more bread with his dinner?
5. What dreary snack does he prepare for himself when he gets home?
6. What does Jacob Marley show Scrooge outside his window?
7. Why does Scrooge's father hate him?
8. Who was Scrooge apprenticed to as a young man?
9. What final humiliation does Scrooge deal this former employer?
10. How long were Scrooge and Marley partners?
11. What excuse does Scrooge keep giving the spirits as to why he can't change?
12. On Christmas morning, what silly thing does he feel he must do?
13. At the end of the movie, what does Scrooge say he doesn't deserve?

ANSWERS: 1. "Silent Night." 2. 7:00 p.m. 3. He helps him with his coat and hat. 4. It costs extra. 5. Porridge (or gruel). 6. A woman holding a baby while spirits hover around her. 7. Because Scrooge's mother died while giving birth to him. 8. Fezziwig. 9. He takes over Fezziwig's business. 10. Eighteen years. 11. "I'm too old." 12. He declares that he must stand on his head. 13. He says that he doesn't deserve to be so happy, but he can't help it.

WHO SAID IT?

Match the line of dialogue with the character who said it. Some characters will be used more than once.

1. "My marriage was the making of me."
2. "Look to see me no more."

A. Ebenezer Scrooge
B. Bob Cratchit
C. Scrooge's fiancee

99

3. "You fear the world too much."
4. "I love you because you're poor."
5. "Is he dead yet?"
6. "It's only once a year, sir."
7. "Christmas, sir, is a humbug."
8. "Mankind was my business."
9. "No--your past."
10. "You've never seen the like of me before."
11. "There's more in life than money."
12. "Never to be lonely again."

D. Fred
E. Fezziwig
F. The Ghost of Christmas Past
G. The Ghost of Christmas Present
H. Jacob Marley

ANSWERS: 1-D, 2-H, 3-C, 4-A, 5-A, 6-B, 7-A, 8-H, 9-F, 10-G, 11-E, 12-A.

MINOR PLAYERS

1. A man approaches Scrooge outside the bank asking for a loan extension. How much has he borrowed?
2. When we first see Tiny Tim, what are he and his mother shopping for?
3. What does Tiny Tim see in a shop window that catches his eye?
4. How much does Scrooge pay Bob Cratchit each week?
5. How many children does Bob have? What are their names?
6. What was the name of Scrooge's sister?
7. Scrooge pays his housekeeper, Mrs. Dilber, two shillings a week. On Christmas Day, what does he raise that salary to?

ANSWERS: 1. Twenty pounds. 2. A goose. 3. Mechanical dolls. 4. Fifteen shillings. 5. Five. Their names are Martha, Peter, Mary, Belinda, and Tim. 6. Fan. 7. Ten shillings.

THE CHRISTMAS SPIRITS

Without those four ghosts, Scrooge wouldn't have a chance. Here are questions about the four ghosts who go above and beyond the call of duty.

1. What does Marley drag around with him?
2. How long has Marley been dead?
3. What is the time on the clock when the ghost of Marley appears?

4. At what time does the Ghost of Christmas Past materialize?
5. In this movie, what does the Ghost of Christmas Past look like?
6. We hear the Ghost of Christmas Present before we see him. What in particular do we hear?
7. When Scrooge touches the robe of the Ghost of Christmas Present, what is he able to do?
8. What are the names of the children beneath the robes of the Ghost of Christmas Present?
9. What is the only part of the Ghost of Christmas Yet to Come not covered in black?

ANSWERS: 1. Chains, cash boxes, and ledgers. 2. Seven years. 3. 10:20 p.m. 4. 1:00 a.m. 5. An old man with long hair. 6. His laughter. 7. Fly. 8. Ignorance and Want. 9. His left hand.

GOING MY WAY

VITAL STATISTICS
Year Released: 1944
Studio: Paramount

Director: Leo McCarey
Writer: Frank Butler and Frank Cavett
Cast: Bing Crosby, Barry Fitzgerald, Rise Stevens, Gene Lockhart,
    and William Frawley

Academy Award Nominations: 10
Academy Award Winners: 7

Claim to Fame: Established Bing Crosby as a real actor and helped to
cement his nice-guy image. One of the most popular--and awarded--
"priest" dramas ever made. Also marked the first and last time a performer (Barry Fitzgerald) was nominated for an Oscar as Best Actor
and Best Supporting Actor for the same role. Academy rules were subsequently changed to prevent that from happening again.

THE STORY

Young priest Father Chuck O'Malley (Bing Crosby) has been assigned
to New York's ailing St. Dominick's parish, led for 45 years by Father

Fitzgibbons (Barry Fitzgerald), a gentle soul somewhat out of touch with the times. It is Father O'Malley's mission to get St. Dominick's out of its financial troubles and strengthen its bond with its parishoners. Father O'Malley becomes the friend of all, including Father Fitzgibbons, a group of neighborhood boys whose gang he turns into a choir, and a pretty runaway he keeps his eye on to keep her from making money the easy way. Meanwhile, he puts his songwriting talents to work, hoping his inspirational song, "Going My Way," will be a hit and bolster St. Dominick's unhealthy bank balance. As it turns out, a light-hearted ditty called "Swinging on a Star" is the hit, and things are looking up. Then the church is consumed by fire, and Father O'Malley learns he is being transferred to another parish. But he still arranges for a special Christmas gift for Father Fitzgibbons before the credits roll.

WHAT THE CRITICS SAID

In *Variety*:
"Topnotch entertainment for wide audience appeal. . . . Picture is a warm, human drama. . . . Intimate scenes between Crosby and Fitzgerald dominate throughout, with both providing slick characterizations."

In the *New York Times*:
"Old Bing is giving the best show of his career. That's saying a lot for a performer who has been one of the steadiest joys of the screen. . . . He has been stunningly supported by Barry Fitzgerald, who plays one of the warmest characters the screen has ever known. . . . They make it one of the rare delights of the year."

BEHIND THE SCENES WITH GOING MY WAY

Going My Way won an Academy Award for Best Picture. It was the first time a Paramount film had won that award since 1927's *Wings*, the very first movie to win an Academy Award for Best Picture.

In addition, the picture won Oscars for Best Actor (Bing Crosby), Best Director (Leo McCarey), Best Song ("Swinging on a Star"), and Best Supporting Actor (Barry Fitzgerald).

Leo McCarey, the director of the film, had a penchant for sentimental films like *Going My Way*. Yet he was also the director of the brilliantly madcap Marx Brothers classic *Duck Soup*. He won three Oscars during the course of his career.

Going My Way made $6 million in its initial release.

The oh-so-Irish combination of Bing Crosby and Barry Fitzgerald (whose real name was plain William Shields, though he really *was* Irish) was so popular that Paramount made another picture starring the pair, 1947's *Welcome Stranger*. Any similarities to *Going My Way* were purely intentional. In the film, Crosby plays a young doctor with new ideas that old curmudgeon doctor Fitzgerald intially resists. Naturally, Fitzgerald is won over in the end (especially when Crosby saves his life in an emergency operation). Critics and audiences alike noticed the similarities between the two scripts (the two films even shared screenwriter Frank Butler), but no one seemed to care. The picture was popular and made money.

As if that weren't enough, Paramount served up more or less the same dish in 1949, when they released *Top o' the Morning*. Going even heavier on the Irish charm than the previous Crosby/Fitzgerald ventures, this one is actually set on the Emerald Isle and again features songs by Jimmy Van Heusen and Johnny Burke. This time, audiences and critics smelled a rat, and *Top o' the Morning* was a flop. There would be no more Crosby/Fitzgerald pairings.

What do *Going My Way* and *Miracle on 34th Street* have in common? A bevy of supporting actors! Porter Hall, William Frawley, and Gene Lockhart appeared in all three. In addition, Gene Lockhart appeared in another Christmas film, 1938's *A Christmas Carol*. William Frawley, of course, was in another Christmas classic, *The Lemon Drop Kid*, and played Fred Mertz in *I Love Lucy*, which boasts a famous Christmas episode in which Lucy, Ricky, Fred, and Ethel have a mysterious encounter with a fellow who just might be the real Santa Claus.

Having real-life opera star Rise Stevens perform *Carmen* wasn't the product of chance. Native New Yorker Stevens was one of the Metropolitan Opera's biggest stars during the 1940s, and the mezzo-soprano's greatest role was widely considered to be Carmen. Her recording of that role is still available on CD.

Going My Way was the film industry's number one moneymaker in 1944.

On the day of the Oscars, Bing was on the golf course and had no intention of attending the ceremonies. His bosses at Paramount felt differently, however, and ordered him off the course so he'd be at the ceremonies on time.

So great was Bing's popularity at the time that when he won the Oscar, he was actually able to convince the Academy to give him two statuettes. One he kept for himself and the other he sent to Gonzaga University, his alma mater in Washington State.

Bing was nominated for playing Father Chuck O'Malley twice! When he played him in *The Bells of Saint Mary's*, the Academy again honored him with a nomination, but this time he lost out to Ray Milland in

Lost Weekend. Bing was nominated for an Oscar a final time for *The Country Girl*, in which he played an alcoholic (not Father Chuck O'Malley). He didn't win, but his costar, Grace Kelly, did.

In 1944, "Swinging on a Star" was a number one hit for Bing for nine weeks. As impressive as that sounds, it was probably no big deal to Bing. That same year, he had six other number one hits, including the Cole Porter classic "Don't Fence Me In."

TRIVIA QUIZZES

BITS & PIECES

1. Which Hollywood studio released *Going My Way*?
2. Who received first billing in the film?
3. What is the name of the parish in the movie?
4. What is Father O'Malley's first name?
5. Who plays the head of the savings and loan that holds the mortgage on the church?
6. What is the name of the savings and loan?
7. What costar of *I Love Lucy* played the music publisher?
8. What disaster befalls the church near the end of the movie?
9. Father O'Malley's friend is pastor at what parish?
10. What is the name of that friend?
11. Father O'Malley sends his boys' chorus on the road to make money for the church. How big a check do they send back?

ANSWERS: 1. Paramount. 2. Bing Crosby. 3. St. Dominick's. 4. Chuck. 5. Gene Lockhart. 6. Knickerbocker Savings and Loan. 7. William Frawley. 8. A fire. 9. St. Francis. 10. Father Tim O'Dowd. 11. $3,500.

FRIENDS AND PARISHONERS

1. What *Our Gang* star played a young hoodlum named Herman?

2. What type of poultry are the neighborhood boys accused of stealing?
3. What three words that pretty runaway Carol James keeps repeating worry   Father O'Malley?
4. How does Tony, the gang leader, get Herman to do what he wants?
5. What does Carol James tell Father O'Malley she'd like to be?
6. What does Father Fitzgibbons advise her to be instead?
7. What is the name by which Father O'Malley knows his friend the opera singer?
8. What stage name has she taken?
9. What opera do we see her perform?
10. What does Father O'Malley give Tony for Christmas?

ANSWERS: 1. Carl "Alfalfa" Switzer. 2. Turkeys. 3. "I'll get by."
4. Slaps him around. 5. A singer. 6. A wife and mother. 7. Jenny Tuffle.
8. Genevieve Linden. 9. Carmen. 10. His baseball jacket.

MUSICAL INTERLUDES

Though it's not a musical, Going My Way *is full of many tuneful interludes. Let's see how many you remember.*

1. How many original songs debuted in *Going My Way?*
2. What song do Carol and Father O'Malley sing together?
3. Father O'Malley tells Carol to sing with more feeling. What else does he criticize?
4. What nursery rhyme is the first song Father O'Malley has the boys sing?
5. What Christmas carol does he teach them?
6. With what "Irish lullaby" does Father O'Malley sing Father Fitzgibbons to sleep?
7. What song does Father O'Malley sing to lovers Carol and Ted to straighten them out?
8. What Father O'Malley composition finally wins the approval of the music publisher?
9. What four animals are mentioned in that song?

ANSWERS: 1. Three. 2. "The Day After Forever." 3. The way she uses her hands when she sings. 4. "Three Blind Mice." 5. "Silent Night." 6. "Too-ra-loo-ra-loo-ral." 7. "Going My Way." 8. "Swinging on a Star." 9. Mules, pigs, fish, and monkeys.

MEET OUR HEROES

1. What is Father O'Malley's favorite baseball team?
2. What is his full name?
3. Why did he stop writing to his friend Jenny?
4. What board game does he play with Father Fitzgibbons?
5. Who wins the game?
6. What holiday does Father O'Malley regretfully tell Father Fitzgibbons he will not spend at the parish?
7. Why will he not be present for that holiday?
8. What does Father Fitzgibbons' mother send him every year for Christmas?
9. Where does he hide that item?
10. What sport does Father O'Malley teach Father Fitzgibbons?
11. What is Father O'Malley's Christmas gift to Father Fitzgibbons?

ANSWERS: 1. St. Louis Browns. 2. Charles Francis Patrick O'Malley. 3. He became a priest. 4. Checkers. 5. Father O'Malley. 6. Christmas. 7. He is being transferred to another parish. 8. A bottle of whiskey. 9. In a music box in his bookcase. 10. Golf. 11. A visit from his mother.

MEET ME IN ST. LOUIS

VITAL STATISTICS
Year Released: 1944
Studio: MGM

Director: Vincente Minnelli
Writers: Irving Brecher and Fred Finklehoffe
Cast: Judy Garland, Margaret O'Brien, Lucille Bremer, Mary Astor,
    Leon Ames, Tom Drake, and Marjorie Main

Academy Award Nominations: 4
Academy Awards Won: 0

Claim to Fame: A landmark movie musical, *Meet Me in St. Louis* was
influenced by the success of Broadway's *Oklahoma!* Like that musical,
the setting is pure Americana and the characters are homespun. And, as
in that Rodgers and Hammerstein musical, director Vincente Minnelli
insisted that the songs flow naturally out of the dramatic situations. He
felt movie musicals should mature past the point where the characters
exclaim, "Hey, kids! Let's put on a show!" in order to introduce a song.
He capitalized on the nostalgia of the original Sally Benson stories by
dividing the movie into four seasons, each introduced by sepia-toned
postcards that delicately change into live action shots. Even the most
sophisticated film critics have praised *Meet Me in St. Louis'* understat-
ed and tasteful sentimentality.

THE STORY

The Smith family is happy with their life in St. Louis, Missouri, in 1903. They eagerly await the arrival of the World's Fair the following spring and keep themselves busy in the meantime with everyday events. The oldest child, Lon, is off to college; teenage sisters Rose and Esther worry about their love lives; and youngsters Agnes and Tootie just enjoying playing and stirring up trouble on Halloween. Then Mr. Smith announces news that he thinks will makes his family happy: he's been asked to head up the New York office of his law firm. After their initial disappointment, the Smiths accept the news, realizing it's better to be together, even in a strange new city. Then, on Christmas Eve, certain events cause Mr. Smith to see things from a new perspective, and he's able to give his family the best Christmas present possible.

WHAT THE CRITICS SAID

In the *New York Times*:
"All these bits of family humor . . . are done in a manner calculated to warm and enthuse your heart. . . . Vincente Minnelli . . . got all the period charm out of the ladies. . . . [W]e confidently predict that *Meet Me in St. Louis* has a future that is . . . bright. In the words of one of the gentlemen, it is a ginger peachy show."

In the *New York Post*:
"At last MGM has gotten around to doing a musical memory book at once rich, tasteful, and a delight to experience."

In *Variety*:
"*Meet Me in St. Louis* is a wholesome story . . . colorful both in background and in its literal Technicolor, and as American as the World Series. . . . [There] are four socko musical highlights. These have been intelligently highlighted and well-paced by director Vincente Minnelli.

Garland achieves true stature with her understanding performance."

BEHIND THE SCENES WITH MEET ME IN ST. LOUIS

The film was originally advertised with the rather flat tagline, "MGM's glorious love story with music." Couldn't that apply to almost any MGM film?

Director Vincente Minnelli had a showbiz background. His parents were vaudevillians, and he was art director of Radio City Music Hall by the time he was 23 years old.

Lucille Bremer, whose first film this was, was previously a Radio City Rockette, like *White Christmas'* Vera-Ellen.

The movie was based on a series of reminiscences called "The Kensington Stories" by Sally Benson, published in *The New Yorker* in 1941 and 1942. Louis B. Mayer liked the wholesomeness of the stories, though other top executives at MGM considered them too episodic to make a good movie. As usual, Mayer won, paying $40,000 for the rights to the stories.

Sally Benson was actually born in St. Louis in 1897 (she was six at the time of the World's Fair) and died in 1972. *Meet Me in St. Louis* was not her only contact with Hollywood. She wrote screenplays for many films, including such wide-ranging projects as *Anna and the King of Siam, Come to the Stable* (another Christmas story), *The Singing Nun*, and *Viva Las Vegas* (yes, the one with Elvis!).

For many years, *Meet Me in St. Louis* was MGM's second-biggest money maker of all time, second behind only *Gone with the Wind*. The two movies share a cast member: Harry Davenport played Dr. Meade in *Gone with the Wind* and Grandpa in *Meet Me in St. Louis*.

Originally the film was to be shot on the Andy Hardy street, but Mayer wanted this to be a big-budget picture, and so the famous St. Louis street was created at a cost of more than $200,000. MGM hired Lemuel Ayers, fresh off his success in Broadway's *Oklahoma!* to design the set. It is a true microcosm of Victorian architecture, containing everything from the Smiths' elegant Second Empire house to the Truitts' more modest Carpenter gothic house.

Van Johnson was originally slated to play John Truitt but bowed out at the last minute. At one time famed "women's director" George Cukor was to head up the film, but when it was decided to make it a musical, producer Arthur Freed, who had been mentoring Vincente Minnelli, chose him, feeling he would bring fresh talent to the look of MGM's musicals.

The only cast member to win an Oscar during their career was Mary Astor, who was honored as Best Supporting Actress for her work in *The Great Lie* in 1941. However, Judy Garland was honored with a special miniature Oscar for her work in *The Wizard of Oz*, just as Margaret O'Brien was honored with the same type of Oscar for her work in *Meet Me in St. Louis*.

Producer Freed, a lyricist himself (his songwriting partner was Nacio Herb Brown, and their songs are featured in another marvelous Freed production, *Singin' in the Rain*), hired the young songwriting team of Hugh Martin and Ralph Blane to write the songs. He wanted the songs to flow naturally out of the situations (he didn't want any "showstoppers") and felt a young team would be more able to do this. Freed also provides the singing voice for Leon Ames in *Meet Me in St. Louis*.

"The Trolley Song" is generally considered one of the finest songs ever to come out of Hollywood, but in 1903 there were no trolleys yet in St.

Louis. And there still aren't mountains in St. Louis, though they can be seen in several scenes.

Freed was in charge of the musical department at MGM (he called it "my own little Camelot"; others called it "the Freed Unit") and was the guiding hand behind such legendary films as *On the Town, Showboat,* and *Annie Get Your Gun.* He had been a vaudeville performer in his youth and always liked to work with talent from New York. His two favorite MGM performers were Gene Kelly and Judy Garland. He did, however, go with the experience of Richard Rodgers and Oscar Hammerstein II when he bought the rights to their song "Boys and Girls Like You and Me," which had recently been cut from *Oklahoma!* If you don't remember hearing that song in *Meet Me in St. Louis,* don't despair. It was cut from *Meet Me in St. Louis,* too. The song was finally slated to go into the Frank Sinatra/Gene Kelly vehicle *Take Me Out to the Ballgame*--but it was cut again. Liza Minnelli, perhaps feeling sorry for this lovely little tune, sometimes adds the songs to her concerts.

Meet Me in St. Louis was re-made in a television version in 1959. The cast included Jane Powell, Jeanne Crain, Walter Pidgeon, Tab Hunter, Myrna Loy, and a very young Patty Duke. In 1989, a new Broadway version surfaced with 10 new songs. It was only a moderate commercial success, and--needless to say--the critics were not especially kind.

Judy Garland was sick of playing teenagers and didn't want to star in *Meet Me in St. Louis.* She was persuaded by Mayer, Minnelli, and Freed. And she was genuinely happy when she saw how beautiful she looked in the rushes (the MGM makeup artist patterned Garland's makeup after Marlene's Dietrich's look). Later, Garland wrote Freed a note apologizing for her initial lack of enthusiasm.

Garland was, by this age, displaying her legendary temperament and insecurity. She was consistently late on the set (she kept everyone waiting for hours to shoot the Christmas ball, costing the studio $40,000). A perturbed Mary Astor stormed into Garland's dressing room one day and said, "Either get the hell on the set or I'm going home!"

Meet Me in St. Louis has its share of continuity errors. When Esther and Tootie sing "Under the Bamboo Tree," Tootie's slippers change from pink to blue. And during the Smith family's Halloween gathering, the cake Katie serves is clearly two layers, yet later on, one of the cut pieces is three layers!

Margaret O'Brien wasn't quite as young at Tootie claims to be (five years old), but she was a very young seven at the time the movie was made. She was so popular that MGM flooded the stores with Margaret merchandise. There were Margaret books, dolls, and even clothing.

TRIVIA QUIZZES

MEET THE SMITH FAMILY

The Smith family is an idealized portrait of life at the turn of the century, but the writers carefully gave each family member distinct personalities. Here's some questions about them.

1. How many children do the Smiths have? Name them.
2. Where is the son going to college?
3. What is John Truitt doing the first time we see him?
4. What are Mrs. Smith and Katie making in the kitchen in the opening scene?
5. What does Tootie do with her "dead" dolls?
6. What is Mr. Smith's profession?
7. When Warren Sheffield calls long distance, what city is he calling from?
8. What does Esther ask John to help her with after the going-away party?
9. How does Tootie "kill" Mr. Brockhurst on Halloween?
10. What is Tootie's injury on Halloween night?
11. What treat does Rose bring home on Halloween?

12. What song do Mr. and Mrs. Smith sing at the piano?

ANSWERS: 1. Five. Alonzo, Jr. (Lon), Rose, Esther, Agnes, and Tootie. 2. Princeton. 3. Standing on his front lawn smoking a pipe. 4. Ketchup. 5. Buries them. 6. He's an attorney. 7. New York City. 8. Turning out all the lights. 9. She throws flour in his face. 10. Her lip is cut. 11. Ice cream. 12. "You and I."

CHRISTMAS ON KENSINGTON AVENUE

After their hectic Halloween, the Smiths were no doubt expecting a nice, quiet Christmas before moving to New York. Unfortunately, it didn't work out that way. Here's a journey through their Christmas mishaps.

1. How many snow people are on the Smiths' front lawn?
2. Who chides the Smith siblings for their lack of Christmas spirit?
3. How many of the Smiths aren't going to the dance with the person they wanted?
4. Why can't John Truitt go to the dance?
5. Who does Katie suggest take Rose to the dance?
6. Who does Grandpa suggest take Esther to the dance?
7. What color dresses do Rose and Esther wear to the dance?
8. Where in the ballroom does Grandpa waltz with Esther to find John?
9. What traditional Scottish song do John and Esther dance to?
10. How does John surprise Esther after the dance?
11. What does Tootie do after Esther sings to her on Christmas Eve?
12. Who barges into the Smith house late on Christmas Eve?

ANSWERS: 1. Six. 2. Katie. 3. Three: Lon, Rose, and Esther. 4. He didn't get to the shop in time to pick up his tuxedo. 5. Lon. 6. Himself. 7. Rose wears green; Esther wears red. 8. Behind the Christmas tree. 9. "Auld Lang Syne." 10. He proposes to her. 11. Runs outside and destroys her snow people. 12. Warren Sheffield.

THE LEMON DROP KID

VITAL STATISTICS
Year Released: 1951
Studio: Paramount

Director: Sidney Lanfield
Writers: Edmund Hartmann, Robert O'Brien, and Frank Tashlin
Cast: Bob Hope, Marilyn Maxwell, Jane Darwell, Lloyd Nolan,
    and William Frawley

Academy Award Nominations: 0
Academy Awards Won: 0

Claim to Fame: Though not a musical, *The Lemon Drop Kid* contains two musical numbers. One of them, "Silver Bells," went on to become one of the most popular Christmas songs ever. It was unique at the time in dispensing with the usual pastoral descriptions of Christmas--snowy hills and sleigh rides--and celebrating instead the sights and sounds of Christmas in the city. Director Sidney Landfield gave the song a nice production that called attention to it, especially given the modest budget of the picture. Sung by Bob Hope and Marilyn Maxwell as they stroll through their neighborhood seeing the sights they describe, the song is peppered throughout the movie's soundtrack, but strangely failed to win even an Oscar nomination.

THE STORY

A small-time con man called the Lemon Drop Kid (Bob Hope) has made a big mistake: his bad racing tip has caused gangster Moose Moran (Fred Clark) to lose $10,000. Moose isn't happy, but the Kid promises that he'll pay Moose back by Christmas Eve. The Kid scurries back to New York City, where he devises a plan: dress up like a street-corner Santa--only in this case, he's the charity. The cops quickly put a stop to that, telling him he needs to collect for an official charity. Then the Kid hits upon his best scheme yet. His old friend Nellie Thursday (Jane Darwell) is temporarily homeless, so the Kid decides to open the Nellie Thursday Home for Old Dolls, an old folks' home, with a little help from his sometime girlfriend, Brainey Baxter (Marilyn Maxwell). Enlisting other small-time crooks, the Kid blankets the city in phony Santa Clauses and has soon made his $10,000. But then slick Oxford Charley (Lloyd Nolan) wants a piece of the action, and the Kid is forced to resort to more trickery. More complications--including a madcap chase sequence--ensue before we are given our happy, Bob Hope ending.

BEHIND THE SCENES WITH *THE LEMON DROP KID*

In an interview in *Remember* magazine, "Silver Bells" songwriters Ray Evans and Jay Livingston related the story of how their masterpiece was composed. According to the two men, they were nervous about writing a Christmas song but were inspired by a little silver bell sitting on Evans' desk. They quickly wrote the song, figuring that once it was used in the film, they'd never hear it again. Luckily, Livingston's wife saved the day, for the song was originally titled "Tinkle Bells," a title that gave her the giggles. The title was changed to "Silver Bells," and it didn't disappear when the movie ended its run. In fact, in its various recorded versions, it has sold more than 150 million copies.

Although Bob Hope (born Leslie Townes Hope) occasionally referred to his British birth, he was actually raised in Cleveland, Ohio. At one time, Hope even owned the Cleveland Indians baseball team.

The 1951 *Lemon Drop Kid* with which we're all familiar is a remake of a 1934 "B" picture directed by Marshall Nelson. Though Hope's version is more popular, some purists maintain that the 1934 film is truer to the wisecracking spirit of the original Damon Runyon story.

The Lemon Drop Kid wasn't the first movie in which Hope played an incompetent gambler. He also starred in 1948's *Sorrowful Jones*, in which he was also involved in bad racetrack tips. *Sorrowful Jones* was a remake of *Little Miss Marker*, a popular Shirley Temple vehicle. In *Jones*, the Shirley Temple role was taken by Mary Jane Saunders, a juvenile actress who failed to make the splash of her illustrious predecessor.

Bob Hope appeared in two films with the female costars of Bing Crosby's most popular holiday movies. In 1946, Hope and Marjorie Reynolds (of *Holiday Inn* fame) starred in *Monsieur Beaucaire*, and in 1953 he and Rosemary Clooney (*White Christmas*) made *Here Come the Girls*.

TRIVIA QUIZZES

BITS & PIECES

1. In what sunny state does the movie open?
2. What does Moose tell the Kid he'll find in his stocking if he doesn't raise $10,000 by Christmas Eve?
3. What kind of dog does he steal a sweater from?
4. Why does he want to borrow $10 from Nellie?
5. When Brainey Baxter hears the Kid knocking on her door, what two things does she hide?

6. Who owns the club where Brainey works?

7. How many days before Christmas does the Kid first play Santa Claus?

8. What does the sign that he carries read?

9. What is the Kid's real name?

10. The Kid says his lawyer is busy helping which president?

11. What does the Kid place on top of the craps tables for the old dolls to sleep on?

12. What song do the street-corner Santas sing on their way to work?

13. Who is the first character to sing "Silver Bells"?

14. Where does the Kid get his old lady disguise?

15. How does the Kid escape from Oxford Charley's men?

16. What does the Kid call the mooing cow in the final scene?

ANSWERS: 1. Florida. 2. His head. 3. A dachshund. 4. To get his clothes out of hock. 5. Her purse and a photo. 6. Oxford Charley's. 7. Seventeen. 8. "Save a Life." 9. Sidney Melbourne. 10. Truman. 11. Wrestling mats. 12. "Jingle Bells." 13. Gloomy Willie. 14. From a store window. 15. On a stolen bicycle. 16. Crosby--as in Bing.

THE BISHOP'S WIFE

VITAL STATISTICS
Year Released: 1947
Studio: Liberty/RKO

Director: Henry Koster
Writers: Robert E. Sherwood and Leonardo Bercovici
Cast: Cary Grant, Loretta Young, David Niven, Monty Woolley,
      Gladys Cooper, and Elsa Lanchester

Academy Award Nominations: 5
Academy Awards Won: 1

Claim to Fame: Features the handsomest, most debonair angel ever in the form of Cary Grant, who is convincing in the otherwordly role. This film was a big hit during 1947 and was nominated for Best Picture. Perhaps because its male stars were both English, many people remember this film as taking place in London--it actually unfolds in New York City, and that city has seldom been portrayed with such a romantic patina. The film also proved popular enough to inspire a remake, 1996's *The Preacher's Wife*, starring Denzel Washington (a pretty handsome angel himself!) and Whitney Houston.

THE STORY

Episcopal bishop Henry Brougham (David Niven) is beset by worries one holiday season. His rich, domineering patroness, Mrs. Harrison (Gladys Cooper), insists that the cathedral Henry is building be a virtual shrine to her dead husband. Henry is obsessed with the cathedral and with pleasing Mrs. Harrison, to the obvious neglect of his other duties, including his wife, Julia (Loretta Young). Henry prays for guidance and is surprised when a man introducing himself as an angel (Cary Grant) appears. Calling himself Dudley to everyone else, the angel passes himself off as Henry's assistant and gets to work paying attention to everything and everybody Henry is ignoring--especially Julia. In fact, Dudley falls in love with Julia. But he puts duty before all and fulfills his mission of helping Henry solve his problem with Mrs. Harrison and the cathedral . . . then Dudley gracefully moves on, as angels are supposed to do.

BEHIND THE SCENES WITH *THE BISHOP'S WIFE*

Cary Grant was reluctant to appear in the picture at all, but was finally persuaded by a salary of $500,000 (he later received a bonus of $100,000 just to stay on the film). This was a phenomenal amount in the 1940s, even by Hollywood standards.

The Bishop's Wife was based on the 1928 novel of the same name by Robert Nathan. Nathan was a prolific writer of the 1920s, 30s, and 40s. Two of his books were turned into movies: *The Bishop's Wife* and *Portrait of Jennie* (starring Jennifer Jones), which also dealt with a supernatural theme. He also wrote the screenplay for the Judy Garland film *The Clock*.

The Bishop's Wife was a pet project of producer Sam Goldwyn (though the film was released by RKO), who had every intention of making it a Christmas classic and giving it a big holiday opening (the film was released on November 13, 1947, just in time for the Christmas movie season). According to A. Scott Berg's biography of the producer, *Goldwyn: A Biography*, Goldwyn may have been the only man in Hollywood--other than Frank Capra, of course--who saw the phenomenal power of *It's a Wonderful Life*. According to Berg, Goldwyn was so impressed with *It's A Wonderful Life* that he rushed into the making of *The Bishop's Wife*, intending to make the transformation of Henry Brougham every bit as touching as that of George Bailey.

Cary Grant was first cast in the role of Henry. Several weeks of shooting ensued under director William Seiter before Goldwyn realized that he didn't like the results. He then had Cary Grant and David Niven switch roles, much to the chagrin of both stars, and also brought in new director Henry Koster.

The melancholy brought to the role of Henry by David Niven was quite genuine. Several weeks before filming began, his wife, Primmie, had died in a freak accident at a party at Tyrone Power's house. The guests had been playing Sardines (an English version of Hide and Seek) in the dark when Primmie opened a door and stepped inside, presuming it to be a closet. It turned out to be a staircase leading to the basement, and she plunged into the darkness. She died of massive head injuries the next day.

Having Cary Grant and David Niven switch roles wasn't the only last-minute change. The role of Julia was originally offered to Teresa Wright (of *Mrs. Miniver* and *Pride of the Yankees* fame). She, however, was pregnant. Jean Arthur was offered the role next, but she turned it down, too. Finally, Loretta Young was cast.

Throughout the filming, Cary Grant remained uncomfortable with the role, the script, and, indeed,the whole movie. He was uncharacteristically difficult to work with, prompting a visit to the set from Sam

Goldwyn. Grant appealed to Goldwyn to remove him from the film, saying, "You want me to be happy, don't you?" to which the no-nonsense Goldwyn replied, "I don't give a damn if you're happy. I just want the movie to be finished."

Cockney boy Cary Grant started his performing career as a circus acrobat and remained proud of his athletic ability throughout his life (his ability to flip is shown to good advantage in several scenes of the film *Holiday*). He was also a bit of a health nut, prompting friend David Niven to say that you never knew when you visited Grant whether you'd be served something awful, like a carrot shake.

Grant was given yet another reason to complain when Henry Koster began shooting *The Bishop's Wife* skating rink sequence. Since Loretta Young couldn't skate well enough to perform some of the twirls and tricks required by the script, Koster decided to get skating stand-ins for both stars, shooting them from a distance. Grant complained that he would have no difficulty mastering the skating moves, but Koster was adamant, and that was the end of that.

Grant's prickly personality had an adverse effect on his less-than-confident costar, Loretta Young. During one scene, Dudley and Julia enter a house and Grant muttered under his breath that if the scene they were shooting was supposed to be taking place during winter there should be frost on the windows. The distracted Young was unable to recover in time to get her next line right, and she flubbed it, complaining that "Cary had me thinking about frost on the windows instead of what I was supposed to say." Grant, however, was an important enough star that shooting was temporarily halted while technicians added that all-important frost to the windows.

Loretta Young had a few peevish moments, too. She insisted that only her right profile be shot. Grant promptly decided that his right side was his best side, too. This clearly made it impossible for Koster to shoot a scene in which the two stars were supposed to be looking into one another's eyes. So he compromised, and had Grant stand behind Young while they both gazed soulfully out a window together. When Goldwyn saw that day's rushes, he was furious, barking, "What happened to my love scene?" Koster explained the profile problem, and Goldwyn made yet another visit to the set. "Is it true," he said to Loretta Young, "that you only want one-half of your face photographed?" Young replied that this was true. "Well, how will you feel when I only pay you half your salary?" he snapped.

Royal Command Performances for England's Royal Family had been regular events since the days of Handel's *Messiah*. But it was only in 1946 that the Royal Family (King George VI, Queen Elizabeth, Princess Elizabeth, and Princess Margaret Rose) began to "command" cinematic performances. In 1947--only the second year of Royal Command Performances for movies--*The Bishop's Wife* was selected to be shown to the Windsors, the first American film to earn that honor. Loretta Young was in attendance and proclaimed herself to be very much in awe of the Queen's poise.

Moviegoers weren't the only ones impressed by Cary Grant's savoir-faire. He once quipped, "Everybody wants to be Cary Grant--even me." Of course, he didn't really need scriptwriters to make him witty. He was once at his agent's office when a telegram was delivered reading, "How old Cary Grant?" Grant promptly wired back, "Old Cary Grant fine. How you?"

TRIVIA QUIZZES

BIT & PIECES

1. Who received first billing in *The Bishop's Wife*?
2. What two crises does Dudley prevent in the opening scene?

3. What does Julia admire in a shop window in the opening scene?
4. What two child actors from *It's a Wonderful Life* are also in this movie?
5. What does Dudley tell everyone his official position is?
6. What is the name of Julia's favorite restaurant?
7. What instrument does Dudley play very well?
8. What does Dudley do with Henry's sermon?
9. What winter sport do Dudley and Julia enjoy together?
10. What is the name of the cabby who tags along?
11. How does Dudley prove to Henry that he really is an angel?
12. What happens to Henry when he tries to leave Mrs. Harrison's house?
13. What little miracle does Dudley perform at the professor's home?
14. What does wealthy Mrs. Hamilton keep reminding Henry about?
15. What does everyone think of Dudley after he leaves?

ANSWERS: 1. Cary Grant. 2. Helps a blind man cross the street and saves a baby in a buggy from being hit by a truck. 3. A hat. 4. Karolyn Grimes (Debby) played Zuzu in It's A Wonderful Life; *Bobby Anderson (a boy in the park) played young George in* IAWL. *5. Henry's assistant. 6. Michel's. 7. Harp. 8. Burns it. 9. Ice skating. 10. Sylvester. 11. Opens a locked door without a key. 12. He is stuck to the chair. 13. He keeps refilling the bottle of sherry. 14. That he owes her his position as bishop. 15. Nothing--they don't remember him at all.*

THE SANTA CLAUSE

VITAL STATISTICS
Year Released: 1994
Studio: Disney

Director: John Pasquin
Writers: Leo Benevenuti and Steve Rudnick
Cast: Tim Allen, Eric Lloyd, Wendy Crewson, Judge Rheinhold, and Peter Boyle

Academy Award Nominations: 0
Academy Awards Won: 0

Claim to Fame: Proved that Tim Allen could carry a major film on his own (he had previously starred in the sitcom *Home Improvement* and provided the voice for Buzz Lightyear in *Toy Story*) and make it a megahit--*The Santa Clause* easily brought in more than $100 million. It was the first successful Christmas movie in which Santa Claus is the main character since 1947's *Miracle on 34th Street*. After all, films such as *Santa Clause: The Movie* had been noticeable flops. *The Santa Clause* also stated, rather unusually, that there has not been just one Santa Claus over the centuries but, rather, a series of men who have been the bearded gift-giver. (*Ernest Saves Christmas* used the same idea a few years earlier.) The thousands of kids who saw *The Santa Clause* didn't seem to be bothered by this twist on the Santa legend one bit.

THE STORY

Scott Calvin (Tim Allen) isn't exactly father of the year. When his son, Charlie (Eric Lloyd), is dropped off at his townhouse on Christmas Eve, it's obvious the little boy is dreading every minute. And sure enough, father and son have a terrible time . . . until, that is, they hear a clattering on the rooftop. It seems the real Santa has landed on Scott's roof and fallen. Charlie talks Scott into not only taking him for a ride in the abandoned sleigh but also into putting on the Santa suit--and at that moment, Scott reluctantly becomes the new Santa. During the next year, he tries hard to resist fulfilling the "Santa Clause," though a delighted Charlie tells anyone who will listen about their Christmas Eve adventures. This leads Scott's ex-wife, Laura (Wendy Crewson) and her new husband, Neal (Judge Rheinhold), to get Scott's visitation rights revoked. Only when Scott surrenders to his destiny as the one and only Santa Claus does he become the kind of father to Charlie that even Laura and Neal can approve of.

BEHIND THE SCENES WITH THE SANTA CLAUSE

An early draft of the script showed the old Santa lying on Scott's front lawn with a broken neck. Since that was too gory, it was decided that he would simply disappear.

To get the right look for Scott Calvin as Santa Claus, the make-up designers studied Norman Rockwell's famous Santa Claus illustrations.

Although *The Santa Clause* supposedly takes place in Illinois, mountains are visible in several scenes that supposedly take place close to home.

As Scott and his son fly through the sky near the end of the *The Santa Clause*, if you look carefully a "hidden Mickey" (Mickey Mouse silhouette) can be seen in the moon.

The scene in which Scott and his son are talking at the zoo was actually filmed at the Toronto Metro Zoo rather than at either of the Chicago-area zoos.

Allen says he was very careful during the filming of both movies to stay "in character" as Santa Claus when on the set since there were so many children around. They played the elves.

In its initial release *The Santa Clause* made $145 million.

TRIVIA QUIZZES

MEET OUR HERO

How much do you really know about Scott Calvin, alias Santa Claus?

1. What does the company Scott works for manufacture? What is the name of the company?
2. What does Scott burn on Christmas Eve?
3. Where does he take Charlie for dinner?
4. What words are on the front of the business card Scott pulls from the old Santa's suit?
5. What is the first gift Scott pulls out of the bag at the first house he visits?
6. After his first Christmas, when is Scott due back at the North Pole?
7. On Christmas morning, how does Scott know that his North Pole experience wasn't just a dream?
8. Once he starts becoming Santa Claus, how many pounds does he gain in one week?
9. What Christmas song does his heartbeat sound like?
10. When he takes Charlie to the zoo, what animals follow them down the path?
11. At the business meeting where he shows up in a sweatsuit, how many desserts does he order? Name them.
12. Which of the reindeer gives Scott a Christmas card on his second

Christmas as Santa Claus?

ANSWERS: 1. Toys; B & R Toys. 2. The turkey. 3. Denny's. 4. "Santa Claus, North Pole." 5. A pair of athletic shoes. 6. On the following Thanksgiving. 7. He's still wearing the red satin pajamas. 8. 45 pounds. 9. "Jingle Bells." 10. Reindeer. 11. Four. Chocolate chip cookies, cheesecake, crème brulee, and a hot fudge sundae. 12. Comet.

FRIENDS & FAMILY

1. What is Neal's profession?
2. What article of Neal's clothing does Scott always ridicule?
3. What type of ladder magically appears on Scott's lawn, to the delight of Charlie?
4. According to the elf Judy, how long did it take her to perfect her hot cocoa recipe?
5. Does she shake or stir the hot cocoa?
6. What sign does Charlie hang on his bedroom door at Laura and Neal's house?
7. What gift does Bernard give Charlie?
8. What gift did Laura dream of getting when she was a little girl?
9. What gift did Neal dream of getting when he was a little boy?
10. At what age did Neal stop believing in Santa Claus?
11. What does E.L.F.S. stand for?
12. What color are the sprinkles on the elves' cheeks?

ANSWERS: 1. A psychiatrist. 2. His sweaters. 3. A Rose Suchak Ladder. 4. 1,200 years. 5. Shakes. 6. "North Pole South." 7. A magic snow globe. 8. The Mystery Date board game. 9. An Oscar Mayer weinie whistle. 10. When he was three years old. 11. Effective Liberating Fight Squad. 12. Silver.

WHO SAID IT?

Match the line of dialogue with the character who said it. Some characters may be used more than once.

1. "I heard a clatter!"	A.	Bernard
2. "Whoa! This guy was huge!"	B.	Scott

3. "You put on the suit--you're the   C.   Neal
    big guy."
4. "Have you ever seen reindeer fly?"   D.   Mr. Whittle
5. "I'm seeing someone in wrapping."   E.   Charlie
6. "Thanks for keeping his feet on   F.   Laura
    the ground."   G.   Judy
7. "You're starting to look like the
    Pillsbury Dough Boy."
8. "You were just denying your
    inner child."

ANSWERS: 1-E, 2-B, 3-A, 4-C, 5-G, 6-F, 7-D, 8-E.

THE SANTA CLAUSE 2

VITAL STATISTICS
Year Released: 2002
Studio: Disney

Director: Michael Lembeck
Writers: Don Rhymer, Cinco Paul, Ken Daurio, Ed Deuter, and
John J. Strauss
Cast: Tim Allen, Elizabeth Mitchell, David Krumholtz, Spencer
Breslin, Eric Lloyd, Wendy Crewson, and Judge Rheinhold

Academy Award Nominations: 0
Academy Awards Won: 0

Claim to Fame: Only two years elapsed between the two *Home Alone* movies; eight years elapsed between the two *Santa Clause* films. This long delay was partly due to star Tim Allen, a stickler for wanting sequels to be just right. He has writers work and rework a script until he likes it--stars can do that sort of thing. (Originally *Toy Story 2* was slated to be released direct to video, but Allen talked producers into making it a first-class production worthy of a theatrical release, and he was proved right.) Critics were generally kind to *The Santa Clause 2* (though many felt it was just an easy way for Disney to make money), and, once again, audiences opened their wallets.

THE STORY

Scott Calvin has adjusted quite well to his new role as Santa Claus. He gives the elves great suggestions on building toys, and he seems to know just what to say to encourage each and every one of them. Of course, there is the little matter of his now-teenage son, Charlie. He's become a bit of a juvenile delinquent in the years that Scott's been Santa Claus, and his uptight school principal, Miss Newman, isn't cutting him any slack. And, as if that problem weren't bad enough, Scott's elves give him some terrible news: in order to stay Santa Claus, he has to get married . . . and he only has a few weeks to find a bride. Since Scott has to leave the North Pole to straighten out Charlie anyway, he decides it can't hurt to look for a bride while he's there . . . and the woman he chooses surprises everybody.

WHAT THE CRITICS SAID

In the *Chicago Sun-Times*:
"*The Santa Clause 2* is more of the same tinsel-draped malarkey that made the original film into a big hit, but it's more engaging, assured, and funny, and I liked it more. . . . The movie is not a special effects extravaganza like The Grinch, but in a way that's a relief. It's more about charm and silliness than about great hulking multimillion-dollar high-tech effects."

In the *London Guardian*:
"Tim Allen reprises his ho-ho-wholly tiresome role as Santa Claus, presiding over an underworld civilisation of toy-making elves, played . . . by children. This time Santa's magical powers are going; he's losing his gut and his beard, "de-Santa-fying." . . . You may find the syllables bah, hum, and bug dancing on your lips."

132

BEHIND THE SCENES WITH *THE SANTA CLAUSE 2*.

Before its release, *The Santa Clause 2* was promoted by Disney with two different subtitles: *The Escape Clause* and *The Mrs. Clause*. Disney dropped both subtitles when the movie was released to theaters.

The Santa Clause 2 made $139 million in its original release.

Tim Allen was hoping to be in Santa Claus make-up for only 25 days of filming--he wound up wearing it for 55 days.

Transforming Allen into Santa Claus each day took the make-up people four hours. The evil Santa's costume was purposely designed out of plastic because it was easier for Allen to put on each day.

The evil Santa Claus says, "You are a strange, sad little man." This is a line (delivered by Buzz to Woody) the filmmakers borrowed from Allen's previous Disney film, *Toy Story*.

The elf village set was created on three soundstages, totaling 90,000 square feet. It was lit by 799 custom-made box lights. No two doors on the set are exactly the same.

On the set, the elf village was referred to as Elfburg. It is supposed to be set under a dome, just like a toy snow globe.

Though you never get a chance to see them, among the buildings in the elf village are a bakery, a barbershop, a candy store, and a shoe store.

The elves who work in the Naughty and Nice center wear black-and-white striped costumes, like prisoners.

Animatronic reindeer are used in tight shots and shots involving actors (such as when Tim Allen actually rides the reindeer). In wider shots, computer-generated reindeer went to work.

David Krumholtz, who played Bernard, thought his character was too sarcastic in the first movie. He asked director Lembeck whether Bernard could be "filled with Christmas spirit" in the sequel, and his wish was granted.

At the beginning of the film, several elves are pulling sleds across town square, yet not one sled leaves tracks in the snow.

Little red-haired Liliana Mumy, who played Neal and Laura's daughter, Lucy, is the daughter of former red-haired child actor Billy Mumy, who played Will Robinson on TV's *Lost in Space*.

Director Michael Lembeck attended Beverly Hills High School with Rob Reiner, Albert Brooks, and Richard Dreyfuss.

TRIVIA QUIZZES

MEET OUR HERO

1. Near the beginning of the movie, Scott has a meeting with what group of people?
2. What new name does he suggest for the Tooth Fairy?
3. How many days does Scott have to find a wife?
4. According to the Easter Bunny, what percent happier are children since Scott became Santa?
5. What's the first sign that he's being de-Santafied?
6. Which reindeer does he choose to take him to visit his family?
7. What is the name of Charlie's little half-sister who suspects Scott may be Santa?
8. What does Scott's date do in the restaurant that embarrasses him?
9. What is Scott doing when a little girl comes up to him telling him what she wants for Christmas?
10. When Scott awkwardly asks Carol for a date, what two foods does he

suggest they go out for?
11. What was Carol's favorite Christmas gift as a child?
12. How does Scott enliven the dreary staff Christmas party?
13. What magically appears above Scott and Carol's heads as they are about to kiss?
14. After he's used up all his magic, who does Scott call on to get him back to the North Pole?

ANSWERS: 1. The Council of Legendary Figures. 2. "The Molinator." 3. Twenty-eight days. 4. 86 percent. 5. He starts losing weight. 6. Comet. 7. Lucy. 8. She stands up and sings a Christmas song. 9. Helping Principal Newman with detention duty. 10. Noodles and pie. 11. A baby doll. 12. By passing out old board games and toys. 13. Mistletoe. 14. The Tooth Fairy.

TROUBLE AT THE NORTH POLE

Life may be more fun at the North Pole since Scott Calvin arrived, but--not surprisingly--it's more complicated, too. Can you remember some of the many things that go wrong during the movie?

1. When the airplane flies over the North Pole in the opening scene, what sound do they hear on their radio?
2. After that, what song do they hear?
3. What is the name of the number two elf? How old is he?
4. What book does the number two elf always carry around, much to Bernard's annoyance?
5. What does Bernard give Scott before he leaves the North Pole?
6. What word does Bernard warn the elves not to say in front of the substitute Santa?
7. What beverage does the false Santa quickly get hooked on?
8. What does Bernard tell the false Santa he needs to stop saying so frequently?
9. What game that Scott taught the elves does the false Santa play a little too roughly?
10. What part of the toy factory does Bernard try to keep the false Santa away from?
11. What does the false Santa create to support him in his efforts to take over the North Pole?
12. What does the false Santa want the children of the world to get for

Christmas?

13. What happens to Bernard when he exposes the false Santa?

14. What is the name of the baby reindeer Scott uses to chase down the false Santa on Christmas Eve?

ANSWERS: 1. Tiny hammers pounding. 2. "Santa Claus Is Comin' to Town," as sung by Smokey Robinson. 3. Curtis; he's 900 years old. 4. The Santa Handbook. 5. A watch that measures how much magic he has. 6. "Plastic." 7. Hot cocoa. 8. "Ho, ho, ho!" 9. Football. 10. The Naughty and Nice Center. 11. An army of giant toy soldiers. 12. Coal. 13. He's dragged away and placed under house arrest. 14. Chet.

WHO SAID IT?

Match the line of dialogue with the character who said it.

1. "Wow! One mistake in 900 years!"	A. Scott as Santa
2. "I think it makes you look hot."	B. Scott as himself
3. "A battle of wits. Too bad you came unarmed."	C. Bernard
4. "Being Santa has made you an even better man."	D. Charlie
5. "You guys aren't elves; you're wizards!"	E. Neal
6. "I got a needlepoint sweater and a minivan!"	F. Curtis
7. "That's one of the perks of my seniority."	G. Carol Newman
8. "I thought you were on my side."	H. Laura
9. "I like rules!"	I. False Santa

ANSWERS: 1-F, 2-E, 3-G, 4-H, 5-A, 6-B, 7-C, 8-D, 9-I.

DR. SEUSS' HOW THE GRINCH STOLE CHRISTMAS

VITAL STATISTICS

Year Released: 2000
Studio: Universal

Director: Ron Howard
Writers: Jeffrey Price and Peter S. Seaman
Cast: Jim Carrey, Taylor Momsen, Jeffrey Tambor, Christine Baranski, Clint Howard, and Molly Shannon

Academy Award Nominations: 3
Academy Awards Won: 1

Claim to Fame: This movie proved that when it's the critics versus Carrey, Christmas, and Seuss, the critics are going to lose. The movie's lukewarm reviews criticized the hectic, almost hysterical, pacing of the picture as well as the filmmakers' departure from the spirit of Seuss' original tale. In this version, most of the Who's are just as mean as the Grinch (and the Mayor is considerably worse). The elaborate production, while admired to a certain extent, was also accused of being overblown and murky-looking. But moviegoers, looking for a new Christmas classic, made this film a box-office smash, and Jim Carrey had another hit on his hands.

THE STORY

"The Grinch hated Christmas," Dr. Seuss tells us. In the book, we are only given the narrator's best guess that the Grinch's dislike of Christmas stems from the fact that his heart was "two sizes too small." In this film, we're given a definite reason: he was terrorized by the Who's as a child. When the movie opens, the Grinch is living a miserable and lonely existence in his mountain home. When kind little Sally Who nominates him as Holiday Cheermeister, the Grinch comes down reluctantly, only to find himself having a fine time. Then the mean tricks start up again, and the Grinch once again returns to his cave with just one thought in mind: revenge! Just how the Grinch steals Christmas and how he is redeemed is played out in glorious Technicolor.

WHAT THE CRITICS SAID

In the *San Francisco Chronicle*:
"Overall, the film sparkles. But it's a curiously unaffecting sparkle, an example, almost, of how the special effects stole Christmas. It goes so far beyond Dr. Seuss' framework of the fanciful that it feels punishing, so fake, revved up and padded out that the human heart that's supposed to be at the story's core is constricted."

In the *Village Voice*:
"*How the Grinch Stole Christmas* would seem to be director Ron Howard's bid for immortality. The movie is intended to be a perennial that will flower at the box office every holiday season. Considerable effort has gone into the production. . . . . The movie is perhaps 20 minutes too long and subject to torpor."

In the *Chicago Sun-Times*:
"This is a movie that devotes enormous resources to the mistaken belief that children and their parents want to see a dank, eerie, weird

movie about a sour creature who lives on top of a mountain of garbage, scares children, is mean to his dog, and steals everyone's Christmas presents. . . . The Grinch is played by Jim Carrey, who works as hard as an actor has ever worked to no avail."

BEHIND THE SCENES WITH HOW THE GRINCH STOLE CHRISTMAS

The film cost $123 million to make and brought in $260 million in its initial release.

Two stars provide off-screen additions to the film: Anthony Hopkins narrates (it was one day's work for him), and Faith Hill sings "Where Are You Christmas?" over the closing credits.

The Whoville set was the largest ever built at Universal Studios, taking up more than 11 sound stages (about 30,000 square feet). The set was partially made of 2 million linear feet of Styrofoam. To make it seem even larger, it was surrounded by a blue-screen "wrap" so that mountains, trees, and skies could be added by computer.

If Whoville looks festive, it's not surprising. More than 8,200 ornaments and 2,000 candy canes were created for the film.

Many of the Who's who merely provide atmosphere (riding bicycles, tumbling, and flipping) are actually members of the Cirque du Soleil.

The snow in the film got its sparkly look in a unique way: it was made of crushed marble.

The set was built not too far from Universal Studios' famous Bates Motel. One day, when not in Grinch makeup, Carrey ran out of the house wearing a dress and waving a knife around. Needless to say, he gave the tourists a good scare, though they didn't realize who it was.

The dog who "plays" Max was new to the world of movies. He was rescued from a pound just four months before shooting began.

Hollywood make-up legend Rick Baker designed the Grinch's makeup as well as that of the Who's. He tested and videotaped several versions of Grinch makeup on himself first. (His hard work paid off; he won an Academy Award for the film.) And he and Jim Carrey weren't the only ones to Grinch themselves. To get a better feel for what Jim Carrey was experiencing, one day director Ron Howard wore full Grinch regalia and directed the entire day in makeup. He surprised Carrey, who was angry at first, thinking there was a new stuntman who looked nothing like him.

It took the makeup crew two-and-a-half hours a day to get Jim Carrey into his makeup and one hour to get him out of the makeup. He wore it for a total of 92 days. He found the experience so trying that, as he put it, he got "very Zen." He also called on the services of a Navy SEAL to teach him torture-resistance techniques.

One thing Carrey never got completely used to were the yellow contact lenses, which covered the entire surface of his eye and were extremely painful. Near the end of filming, he quit wearing them completely. In these scenes, the yellow color in his eyes was added in post-production.

According to Rick Baker, Carrey's facial apparatus was tissue-thin in some places to take advantage of his expressive face. In some places, only makeup was used, though there was not one "Grinch green"; rather, a mix of green, brown, and purple makeup gave the Grinch his peculiar skin.

All the sweaters in the movie were hand-knit by three people. That's a lot of knitting! Altogether 250 sweaters were worn in Whoville. These were just part of the 450 costumes created for the film.

The rest of the Who's wore an apparatus made up of a nose and an upper lip. Baker worked for a long time to duplicate the look of Seuss' Who's without having them look like the creatures in the "Eye of the Beholder" episode of *The Twilight Zone* where everyone looked like a pig. Some Who's also wore dentures, ears, and wigs.

On a busy day, more than 45 makeup artists were working at one time.

The entire movie was designed with swirls and curves, to resembles Dr. Seuss' artwork. In several scenes, the clouds spell out the intials R.H. (director Howard), J.C. (star Carrey), and C.H. (Clint Howard, the director's brother as well as the man who plays the Mayor's sidekick, Whobris).

Other Ron Howard relatives also appear in the film. Howard's father shouts, "Put him in the Chair of Cheer!" during the Whobilation, and Howard's wife and red-haired daughter both show up in the final scene. Howard himself (in Who makeup) also makes a cameo in the city square in one scene. The film is dedicated to the memory of Howard's mother, "who loved Christmas the best," according to the on-screen dedication.

When Max and the Grinch get in the Dumpit to Crumpit, Max's collar is missing. By the time they arrive back at the mountain, it's back on his neck.

Audrey Geisel, the widow of Theodore Geisel (Dr. Seuss) had been approached several times for permission to make a film version of her husband's famous Christmas story and was only convinced when she saw a stage production of the book in San Diego. She visited Carrey on the set of *The Man in the Moon* before approving him to play the

Grinch. Art director Michael Curenbith said Whoville captures the spirit rather than the letter of Seuss' drawings. In the book, only a few "haystack" houses are shown, and Curenbith knew he had to go beyond that. In looking at other Seuss books, he noticed that Seuss made use of the swirling minarets of Moroccan and Islamic architecture, and Curenbith added those elements to his conception of Whoville.

The village itself was planned to look like a medieval village, with the tree being the very center of the town. Audrey Geisel declared the finished product to be "perfect."

During the Whobilation, the Grinch can be seen jumping into someone's arms after he sets the tree on fire. In the next shot, he's still standing next to the tree.

Producer Brian Grazer bought the rights to *The Cat in the Hat* at the same time he bought the rights to *The Grinch*. The success of the first film persuaded him to put the other Seuss title on the big screen, and it came to theatres in Christmas 2003. Though successful, it was not the blockbuster *The Grinch* had been.

TRIVIA QUIZZES

MEET OUR HERO (?)

You know he's green, and you know he hates Christmas. Let's see how much you know about the 2000 edition of the Grinch.

1. What is the name of the mountain where the Grinch makes his home?
2. What color is his front door?
3. At the beginning of the movie, what is he munching on?
4. On what day of the year was the Grinch "born"?
5. When his foster mothers offer him Christmas treats as a child, what does he choose?
6. As a child, what Christmas present does he make for Martha May?

7. How old was he when he left Whoville forever?
8. When he sneaks into the Whoville post office, what undesirable piece of mail does he put in most of the post office boxes?
9. What does Cindy Lou insist the Grinch be elected?
10. When the Grinch comes to the Whobilation celebration, what is he wearing?
11. What gift do his foster mothers give him during the ceremony?
12. What gift does the mayor give him?
13. What Whoville decoration does the Grinch set on fire in revenge?
14. What does he say he's doing at the end of the movie when he cries?

ANSWERS: 1. Mount Crumpit. 2. Green. 3. A raw onion. 4. Christmas Eve. 5. He eats the plate the cookies are served on. 6. An angel. 7. Eight. 8. Jury duty notices. 9. Holiday Cheermeister. 10. German lederhosen. 11. A sweater with a light-up Christmas tree. 12. A razor. 13. The Christmas tree. 14. "Leaking."

ALL THE WHO'S DOWN IN WHOVILLE

In Ron Howard's movie, considerable time is spent on detailing life down in Whoville. Here are some details you should remember.

1. What is the name of Whoville's mayor?
2. What does Cindy Lou's dad do for a living?
3. What is the name of Cindy Lou's mother?
4. What is the name of the town's best department store?
5. What is the name of the garbage chute the town's citizens use?
6. What song does Cindy Lou sing in her bedroom?
7. How are baby Who's delivered?
8. What does the school uniform in Whoville resemble?
9. What kind of ride does the Holiday Cheermeister traditionally take?
10. What kind of race is run at the Whobilation?
11. What are the nonsense words that open the Who Christmas song "Welcome, Christmas"?
12. All of tiny Whoville is contained inside what?

ANSWERS: 1. Augustus May-Who. 2. Postal carrier. 3. Betty Lou. 4. Farfingle's. 5. Dumpit to Crumpit. 6. "Christmas, Why Can't I Find You?," a version of "Where Are You Christmas" sung over the closing credits. 7. In special umbrellas called pumbersellas. 8. Sailor suits. 9. A ride on the Chair or Cheer. 10. Sack race. 11. "Fah Who Foraze, Yah Who Doraze." 12. A snowflake.

STEALING CHRISTMAS

In only a few hours, the Grinch manages to strip the town bear. From the time he arrives in town to the time the sun comes up, let's see what you remember.

1. What does the license plate on the Grinch's sleigh read?
2. What part of his reindeer costume does Max reject?
3. Whose house does the Grinch go to first?
4. How does he destroy the stockings at the first house?
5. How does he gather up most of what he steals?
6. When Cindy Lou, thinking he's Santa, asks him what Christmas is all about, what is his answer?
7. What Who pet gets in his way several times as he's stealing Christmas?
8. What does he steal from Martha May's house?
9. What "gift" does Max give the Mayor?
10. What happens that makes leaving Whoville difficult?
11. How many feet up the mountain does Max have to pull the sleigh?
12. What does the Grinch attach the Mayor's bed to?

ANSWERS: 1. Mean 1. 2. The red nose. 3. Cindy Lou's. 4. With a flock of moths. 5. With a giant vacuum. 6. "Vengeance!" 7. A fluffy white cat. 8. The engagement ring the Mayor gave her. 9. A kiss (he licks his face). 10. The Grinch runs out of gas. 11. 3,000 feet. 12. A police car.

WHO SAID IT?

Match the line of dialogue to the character who said it. Some answers will be used more than once.

1. "You some kind of wild animal?"
2. "One's mans toxic sludge is another man's potpourri."
3. "Maybe you need a timeout."
4. "There's no check."
5. "Invite the Grinch; destroy Christmas."

A. Betty Lou Who
B. The Mayor
C. The Grinch
D. Martha May
E. Lou Who
F. Cindy Lou Who

144

6.   "I'm glad he took our presents."
7.   "Merry Christmas, you hunk of burnin' Who."
8.   "Those lights match your outfit perfectly."
9.   "Who wants the gizzard?"

ANSWERS: 1-C, 2-C, 3-F, 4-B, 5-B, 6-E, 7-A, 8-D, 9-C.

THE GATHERING

VITAL STATISTICS
Year First Broadcast: 1977
Network: ABC

Director: Randal Kleiser
Writer: James Poe
Cast: Edward Asner, Maureen Stapleton, Gregory Harrison,
    Stephanie Zimbalist, Lawrence Pressman, Veronica Hamel,
    and Bruce Davison

Emmy Award Nominations: 5
Emmy Awards Won: 1

Claim to Fame: The only made-for-television Christmas movie that deserves to be mentioned with the best holiday films. *The Gathering* also served as the launching pad for the careers of several young television stars: Gregory Harrison (*Trapper John, M.D.*), Stephanie Zimbalist (*Remington Steele*), and Veronica Hamel (*Hill Street Blues*). Even Edward Winter (Colonel Flagg on *M*A*S*H*) is seen briefly in the role of Roger, the boyfriend of Adam Thornton's daughter Peggy.

THE STORY

Self-made millionaire Adam Thornton (Edward Asner) has sacrificed everything--including a happy family life--in his pursuit of success. Now approaching old age, he is alone and content with the choices he has made. Then, a few short weeks before Christmas, his doctor tells him that he is dying, and Adam decides to mend fences in the hope that he will once again see his four children. Aided by his forgiving wife, Kate (Maureen Stapleton), invitations go out to all his children, now grown and scattered. Their reactions are mixed, from surprise to anger to bewilderment. On Christmas Eve, Adam waits nervously, hoping for the doorbell to ring. He especially wants to see his youngest son, a draft evader, whom he hasn't spoken to since their bitter disagreement over the Vietnam War. As the children and grandchildren start arriving, Adams turns to Kate and says, "It's happening!" The man who had walked away from happiness finds himself giving happiness to his long-lost family.

BEHIND THE SCENES WITH THE GATHERING

The Gathering was filmed in Chagrin Falls, Ohio. Chagrin Falls was founded as a milltown but has been known for many decades for its nearby waterfalls, charming Victorian homes, art galleries, and shops.

The movie was first broadcast on December 4, 1977.

The Gathering was a Hanna-Barbera Production, a company not usually associated with serious drama. They are better-known, of course, for producing the animated sitcoms *The Flintstones* and *The Jetsons*.

Adam Thornton's grandchildren, Tiffany and Joey, were played by real-life brother and sister Maureen and Ronald Readinger.

147

Director Randal Kleiser also made two other classic 1970s television movies: *Dawn: Portrait of a Teenage Runaway*, starring Eve Plumb of *The Brady Bunch*, and *The Boy in the Plastic Bubble*, starring a very young John Travolta.

Edward Asner came a long way, careerwise, to star in a classy television movie like *The Gathering*. His very first TV movie was 1965's *The Satan Bug*.

Veronica Hamel (Helen Thornton) came to Hollywood after a long career as a model in New York City. Her good looks got the attention of producer Aaron Spelling, who offered her a role as one of the original *Charlie's Angels*. The serious Hamel chose to play Joyce Davenport on *Hill Street Blues* instead.

The Gathering was nominated for five Emmys: Outstanding Special, Outstanding Actress in a Special (Maureen Stapleton), Outstanding Director (Randal Kleiser), Outstanding Writing (James Poe), and Outstanding Art Direction.

Oddly, *The Gathering's* touching musical score by John Berry, which tugs at your heartstrings at all the right moments, wasn't even nominated for an Emmy, even though there were only four nominees in the music category that year (there could be up to five nominees).

Of its five nominations, it won only the big one: Outstanding Special, beating out competition *Jesus of Nazareth*, *A Death in Canaan*, *Our Town*, and *Young Joe: The Forgotten Kennedy*.

Maureen Stapleton lost the Emmy to Joanne Woodward, making one of her occasional forays into television, for the movie *See How She Runs*.

Although Ed Asner wasn't even nominated for his performance as Adam Thornton, he won an Emmy that year anyway, as Best Actor in his series *Lou Grant.*

In fact, between his series work (*The Mary Tyler Moore Show* and *Lou Grant*) and appearances in mini-series and TV movies, Ed Asner has won seven Emmys.

On December 17, 1979, *The Gathering, Part II*, also a Hanna-Barbera Production, was broadcast--but on NBC, not ABC. This movie tells the story of Kate Thornton taking over the family business and being wooed by Efrem Zimbalist, Jr., a wealthy industrialist who wishes to buy Thornton Industries. Stephanie Zimbalist, his real-life daughter, did not reprise her role as Toni, nor did Gregory Harrison reprise his role as Bud (Toni's husband). Their roles were taken by Patricia Conwell and Jameson Parker. Tiffany and Joey were played by new children, who were not real-life brother and sister. The rest of cast returned to their original roles--all, that is, except Gail Strickland. Her character, Peggy, disappeared altogether.

TRIVIA QUIZZES

BIT & PIECES

1. In what category did *The Gathering* win its Emmy?
2. Who is Adam talking to when the movie begins?
3. How many children do Adam and Kate have?
4. How many grandchildren?
5. What is their youngest son's nickname?
6. What does their youngest son call himself and why?
7. To what U.S. president does Adam sarcastically compare son Tom?
8. To what star of *Boys' Town* does Tom compare his father?
9. What does Adam's doctor give him for Christmas?
10. What do Adam's grandchildren request that he read to them?

11. Where do Adam and Kate find all the Christmas decorations?
12. What is hanging in daughter Peggy's office?
13. What were her original Christmas plans?
14. What does Adam say he can't name even one of?
15. What two presents does Tom switch?
16. Which of Adam's children leaves first?

*ANSWERS: 1. Outstanding Special. 2. His doctor. 3. Four 4. Three.
5. Bud. 6. Steve Smith--he's a draft dodger living under an assumed name
in Canada. 7. Kennedy. 8. Spencer Tracy. 9. Fireworks. 10. "A Visit from
St. Nicholas." 11. In the attic. 12. A picture of the family home. 13. A ski
trip. 14. The stars in the sky. 15. A fishing pole and some liquor.
16. Peggy.*

JINGLE ALL THE WAY

VITAL STATISTICS
Year Released: 1997
Studio: Twentieth-Century Fox

Director: Brian Levant
Writers: Randy Kornfield
Cast: Arnold Schwarzenegger, Jake Lloyd, Sinbad, Phil Hartman,
 Rita Wilson, James Belushi, Martin Mull, and Robert Conrad

Academy Award Nominations: 0
Academy Awards Won: 0

Claim to Fame: Arnold Schwarzenegger was known for action films such as *The Terminator* and *Conan the Destroyer* and energetic comedies such as *Twins* and *Junior*. He had also made one movie with kid costars, *Kindergarten Cop*, though most moviegoers felt the emphasis in that movie was more on the cop than the kindergarten. In *Jingle All the Way*, he found a script that combined all three genres. Though skewered by critics and only moderately successful in its first release, the film nevertheless hits home with a sad truism: for many parents, Christmas is merely a frantic race to get that one toy that manufacturers have convinced kids they can't live without. Ironically, the film failed to sell many of the Turbo Man Action figures that showed up in stores during Christmas 1997.

THE STORY

Howard Langston (Arnold Schwarzenegger) is more devoted to his career than to his wife, Liz (Rita Wilson) or his son, Jamie (Jake Lloyd). So it's no surprise that not only did he not know the name of Jamie's favorite action hero, Turbo Man--he didn't even remember Liz asking him to purchase the very popular action figure. When a guilty Howard finally goes shopping on Christmas Eve morning, he is met with ridicule and derision by store employees everywhere. His only "ally" is another harried father, postman Myron Larrabee. Myron, too, will do anything to get his son a Turbo Man action figure. The two men battle enthusiastically around Minneapolis all day Christmas Eve, until things come to a climax during the city's Wintertainment parade. There, Howard gets a chance to prove to Jamie--and the whole city-- that he really is a hero.

BEHIND THE SCENES WITH *JINGLE ALL THE WAY*

Jingle All the Way wasn't Arnold Schwarzenegger's first Christmas movie. Previously, he had directed a 1993 made-for-TV remake of the Barbara Stanwyck film *Christmas in Connecticut*. His version starred Dyan Cannon and Kris Kristofferson.

Jingle All the Way was produced in part by Chris Columbus, who previously directed the *Home Alone* movies.

The name of Chris Columbus' production company is, appropriately enough, 1492 Productions.

Columbus says he was inspired to make the movie when he spent one Christmas season desperately searching for a Buzz Lightyear doll for his child.

Although the film is set mostly in Minneapolis, Mickey's Dining Car (where Howard and Myron are resting when they hear the radio contest) is actually in downtown St. Paul.

The film's Christmas parade was filmed on Universal Studios' New York Street in the middle of July. It took three weeks in all to film, and most of the time the temperature hovered at around 100 degrees, while actors and extras were bundled up in clothing appropriate for Minnesota. More than 1,500 extras were used.

Among the real-life marching bands that appear in the parade: the UCLA marching band and the Pasadena City College marching band.

Many other scenes actually were filmed in the Twin Cities. Among the neighborhoods used were Linden Hills, Edina, Nicollette Island Park, and Rice Park.

The mall scenes were filmed at Minneapolis' 4.2 million-square-foot Mall of America, with a good part of this sequence being filmed at the mall's enormous Legoland.

In a scene cut from the film, Howard follows a woman out of a toy store when he sees a box with the words Turbo Man peeping from her shopping bag. He offers her a great deal of money for the toy and she rewards him with her phone number and the bag. Only after she walks away does Howard discover that he has just purchased Booster, Turbo Man's nerdy sidekick.

Jake Lloyd, the young actor who played Jamie Langston in *Jingle All the Way*, went on to play a very young Darth Vader in *Star Wars, Episode I: The Phantom Menace*.

In the movie, the character played by Phil Hartman tells Howard, "You won't be able to bench-press your way out of this one"--a sly reference to Schwarzenegger's body-building prowess.

The filmmakers figured that shooting in Minnesota in the winter would guarantee cold weather--not so. The crew spent time adding frost to windows and snow to driveways. However, in some outdoor scenes--particularly in Howard's neighborhood--green, leafy trees can be seen just down the street.

The Turbo Man suit Schwarzenegger wore in the film's final sequence can be seen at Planet Hollywood at Minnesota's Mall of America.

In one scene, Phil Hartman's character asks Howard whether he has put chains on his tires yet. In real life, it would be a moot point, as tire chains are illegal in Minnesota.

TRIVIA QUIZZES

HOWARD'S FRANTIC CHRISTMAS

1. With what words does Howard end all his phone calls at work (even to Liz)?
2. What color karate belt does Jamie currently have and what is he promoted to?
3. What is the name of Turbo Man's sidekick, an annoying pink tiger? What is the name of Turbo Man's archenemy?
4. What is the name of the parade Liz and Jamie go to each year?
5. How much does Howard pay for the Spanish-speaking (and broken) Turbo Man he buys from the unscrupulous mall Santa Claus?
6. How many face-to-face encounters does Howard have with the police officer played by Robert Conrad?
7. What unusual pet does Ted buy to make his son's Christmas really special?
8. What kind of cookies does Ted help Liz bake on Christmas Eve?
9. What toy does Myron Larabee say he always wanted for Christmas and never got?

10. What are the call letters of the radio station running a contest whose prize is a Turbo Man doll?
11. What trivia question do listeners have to answer to win the doll?
12. What is in the first package Myron claims is a mail bomb?
13. According to Liz, Howard is "adamant" about putting what ornament on their Christmas tree each year?
14. Howard kicks the burning head of which of the three Magi out the window of Ted's living room?
15. What drink does Ted offer Liz when they're sitting in his van at the parade?

ANSWERS: 1. "You're my number one customer." 2. He is promoted from yellow to purple. 3. Booster and Dementor. 4. Wintertainment Parade. 5. $300. 6. Five. 7. A real reindeer. 8. Sugar cookies. 9. A Johnny 7 OMA Gun. 10. KQRS 92. 11. They have to name all of Santa's reindeer. 12. A music box. 13. The star. 14. Balthazaar. 15. Nonalcoholic eggnog.